This So-Called Single Life

Sharee A. Smith

This So-Called Single Life

Copyright © 2020 by Mrs. Sharee Antoinette Smith

All rights reserved. No part of this book may be reproduced or transmitted in any form or by any means without written permission of the author.

ISBN: 9798603817682

To Jerron Rashad Smith

Aka "Babe"…My husband, lover, and best friend; thank you for loving me and my children without conditions. Because of your unconditional love, I can smile again, my children can smile again. When I thought about giving up on love, you stepped in and swept me off my feet. You stepped up to care for my children who needed to feel a father's love. I never imagined someone loving us the way you have loved us. Witnessing your selfless acts of love never cease to amaze me. Our love has been tested since we started this journey, but we have stayed afloat in the face of adversities and our enemies! You are truly a man after God's own heart. #AlwaysandForever

To Meshai, Shemia, and CJ

Aka "Three Amigos"…Where would I be in this thing called "life" without you? Thank you for tagging along throughout this journey. It's been one hell of a ride, but we are still here!!!

To Chiquita Jones

My mother and friend; I want to thank you for your continued support and always having my back no matter how many times I let you down. I know I will always be your baby and you will always be my day-1'! Love You!!! Your one and only "Sherry"!

To Floyd Rounds Sr.

My Dad; my Superman! I want to thank you for always being brutally honest with me. Thank you for all the hour lectures on life whenever I was in trouble. I learned so much just from listening to *you talk. I have been able to put all that knowledge you dropped to use in my adult life. I appreciate you for who you are. Love you Dad!*

Acknowledgments

I would like to send a special shout out of thanks to Mrs. Mable Landry for her tireless effort with editing this masterpiece. Her constructive critiques, expertise in English and grammar, encouragement, integrity, and honesty helped me to birth this dream and vision of writing my book.

I would also like to send a very special thanks to Ms. L'Oréal Leaks for her amazing cover artwork. She asked me what I wanted the cover to look like and she delivered this beautiful work of art for my cover. If you want to view more of her artwork, please follow her on Instagram: @lil_lo_loraine

I must thank Lynette Winters for mentoring me through this book writing process. She also assisted me with the formatting the book and marketing tips.

Foreword

By

Mrs. Mable Landry

People so often forget that the answer for today's challenges, distractions, and obstacles is Jesus Christ and the church; the Institute He left as a refuge for the lost, destined, and confused. Satan knows this, so he is always present, as the word says "Be sober, be vigilant; because your adversary the devil, as a roaring lion, walketh about, and seeking whom he may devour. (I Peter 5:8) What great pleasures he gets from exhibiting his true nature. For he is the author of confusion, father of lies, and a shrewd destroyer.

However, according to the scripture Romans 8:28,"And we know that all things work together for good to them that love God, to them who are the called according to his purpose." (Romans 8:28) The fact that God's infinite plan and purpose for one's life can sometimes take one to and through a destiny that one would never consider for themselves, can be mind-blowing and absolutely overwhelming. Innocently we fall in love with God and offer ourselves to be used by Him in any way, shape, or form. However, He so desires.

Yet, there is little knowledge about what the outcome of that offer will bring. In this book, *This So-Called Single Life* is the plight of a young and innocent woman of God who journeyed into life's endeavors. At one time in her life she thought she had it all together, all planned out, and all sewed up. In her mind when one thing did not work, she simply moved on to the next. Little did she know that her thoughts were not God's thoughts, nor was her plans his plans, nor her mind His mind. "For my thoughts are not your thoughts, neither are your ways my ways, saith the Lord." (Isaiah 55:8) "For I know the thoughts that I think toward you, saith the Lord, thoughts of peace, and not of evil, to give you an expected end." (Jeremiah 29:11)

I met Sharee Smith and her family some years ago when my family became members of a church she formally attended. I don't remember the exact capacity in which she served, but I do remember it was in a leadership status. I remember admiring the smiles on their faces as well as the warm and inviting ways in which they welcomed and encouraged us to be a part of their congregation. As growing members of the church, I observed the great respect and appreciation my Bishop and Pastor had for them and vice versa. This was the same spirit so prevalent throughout the leadership of that church and the congregation.

As time passed, Sharee and I grew up in the admonishment and grace of God as He saw fit. I am proud to have been in the presence of this woman of God and her family, both former and present. I am elated to be asked to stand by her as God introduce her to other young Christian men and women who would find themselves in her situations. My prayer is that through the lights of sharing many years of her plight; some lost and wandering child of the Most High God would find their way and be set free from bondage. I think of her as liken to the man the bible speaks of in Matthew 7:24- 25. "I will liken him unto a wise man, which built his house upon a rock: And the rain descended, and the floods came, and the winds blew, and beat upon that house; and it fell not: for it was founded upon a rock.

The rock symbolizes a solid foundation and when the wind and rain came it was able to survive. The house symbolizes life. In life there are things that affect the heart, mind, body and soul. These are given by God to use for serving Him. Sometimes life takes one through some rough times. Sometimes challenges are rough enough to tear one apart, but as long as life is built on the solid foundation of God's statues, principles, and laws; He will make a way of escape. Sometimes, renovations like moving some things out or tearing some things down has to be done. Sometimes one has to do some remodeling in which the entire structure of the house has to be revamped. Whichever needs to be done, one has just do it, but without changing the foundation. One has to hold on to that solid foundation for without it, guess who's there to capture the win.

Friends may get to be few and some you may lose along the way. But guess what, Jesus is always there, and He really cares for you. Sharee's dream has always been to help others by telling her story. I am so glad she is determined to persevere and fight the good fight of faith. I hope and pray you are encouraged by her story.

Preface

When you look back over your life, do you ever think that you have a story to tell? Do you have any regrets about any choices you've made from the time you were old enough to decide until your present age? If you were given the opportunity, would you go back and "re-do" life or do somethings all over again? These are questions I would ask myself from time to time before I sat down to write this book. As I reflected over my life, I realized I had a story to tell. Everything I'd gone through from my childhood, my teenage years, and my first marriage, all were setting me up for my unexpected blessing. I had to go through "the process" for God to get the glory out of my life. All the heartache, heartbreak, and turmoil I experienced was God preparing me to tell my story, my truth. There were times when I thought I wasn't going to make it. Times that I wanted to give up, throw in the towel, and walk away from it all! It wasn't until I sat down to write this book that God gave me the understanding and revelation of why I must share my life experiences with the world. Even though God gave me an understanding of why I had to write this book, I still questioned Him on some things. They are experiences that made me ashamed and embarrassed. These experiences were filled with a lot of guilt and regret. As I wrote, God let me know that He was freeing me from my past and the stigma that so many people who crossed my path held me to. He stated that He was rewriting my story for His glory!

I used to be very timid and shy, afraid to speak my mind, hiding in the background of those I looked up to and always worried about what others thought of me. My self-esteem was very low, lacking the confidence that God gave me. As you read, I pray you can find strength in my story, encouragement, and that you are blessed through my testimony.

My parents were born and raised in St. Louis, Missouri. They attended the same school and became high school sweethearts shortly after they met. Mom was the youngest of eight siblings. My grandmother was a single parent who raised her children in the admonition of God and made sure to instill the things of God in their hearts. Proverbs 22:6 says, train up a child in the way he should go: and when he is old, he will not depart from it. Her decision to live a saved and sanctified life in front of them, made a difference as to how they turned out as adults. My mom and I lived in a house together with my grandmother, aunties, and cousins. My grandmother watched us while our mothers went to school and work. Every single day she fixed us breakfast, sat us at the table, and read the bible to us. And after our bible study lessons, she would pray over us. My grandfather was a preacher and I loved him dearly. He presented my first bible to me when I was about seven years old. He told me to make sure I read it every day because it was going to help me in life. He too, seriously admonished the word of God in his children's life.

As a little girl growing up, my father was my "Superman", and he was everything to me! His parents raised him, along with his siblings in a loving environment, even though they didn't know much about going to church. I can't recall my dad ever mentioning much about his father. My grandmother on the other hand, he loved with all his heart and talked about a lot. She had a very stern demeanor. Dad always told me stories of how she would scold them when they were disobedient. It was very hard to believe Dad when he talked about my grandmother and how tough she was at times, because she was short in stature and had a thin body frame! And when it came to discipline, she did not "play the fiddle"! Her affection and love were expressed differently, not always through a hug or a kiss on the cheek. Later on, in life, I understood why it was so difficult for my dad to show affection to my siblings and me.

My ears were always eager to hear the stories my mom shared with me about my dad. One story she shared with me is how my dad would flirt with girls at school, including her. From the way she talked about him, he was quite the ladies' man! Mother expressed how they met with excitement! The party they went to was the beginning of something special. It was from there that sparks begun to fly! They dated for three years before Mother gave birth to me and decided to marry shortly after. According to Mother, the marriage began to diminish, because of indifferences and outside interference from others. She felt that infidelity had crept in, spawning a divorce by the time I turned three years old. After the divorce, she decided to leave Missouri and enlist in the Air Force, leaving me in the care of my dad.

Things were going great with Dad and me for about a year and a half, until Mother felt that I needed to be with her. She had planned to have me escorted to her by my aunt. She told my aunt to not worry about packing clothes for me because she had everything I needed. Her main concern was making sure she had me safely in her care. The perfect opportunity arose for her to execute her strategy the day of my cousin's birthday party. The airline tickets were sent to my aunt. My dad dropped me off at the party. He gave me the biggest hug and kiss a father could give his little girl, hopped in the car, and drove off.

My aunt waited until my dad was out of sight before we headed to the airport. We flew to Texas to meet my mom. I didn't quite know what was going on, but I felt the excitement inside because I was getting ready to see my mom. My aunt got back on another plane after she delivered me to my mom and headed back to St. Louis. Mom and I headed to her home in Albuquerque, New Mexico. Once my dad found out what had taken place, he was furious, hurt, and dismayed with my mom and her family! He couldn't believe that she would ever take me away from him. In my heart of hearts, I felt this one bad decision is what caused my dad to have feelings of distrust for years to come. For a long time, I felt as if his hurting heart was directed towards me. Well maybe not directly, but it appears I had to pay for her devious intentions with our relationship. Our daddy-daughter bond suffered because of the pain my mother caused my dad when she took me from him.

Three years later the news came that my mom would have to work overseas. She received a three-year assignment to go to Seoul, Korea. She wanted to take me with her, but Dad was not having it at all! He did not want his seven-year-old daughter leaving him for three years to go out of the country. They both decided it was best I come to St. Louis to live with him and his new wife. Although I first met my stepmother when I was just a little baby, I was too young to remember anything about her. I didn't really get to know her until I moved in with them after my mom left to go overseas. I had to learn to adapt to this new life living with my dad, stepmom, and my newborn baby brother. My whole world that I once knew, had changed. It changed from being an only child for seven years and having a mother who did everything for me, to having to learn to do certain things on my own. The hardest part was having to learn to share my dad with my brother. I went through a lot of issues and experienced a lot of turmoil with my stepmother. Every time Mother called, I begged her to come back to the states and get me so that I could live with her again. This is how I got the opportunity to travel a lot between my parents until I was old enough, to decide which one I wanted to stay with.

Eventually, I went to live with my mom, and it wasn't because I loved my dad any less. I felt like it was better for my mom and I to be together, yet I missed my dad tremendously. Throughout my high school years, I became very promiscuous. I would say it was not by choice, but I'm not sure if this is a totally true statement. Sometimes I felt as if I had to do it to feel the love and acceptance I longed for from my father. At other times, it was my own lustful desires that pushed me to fulfill the needs of my flesh. I was very adamant about trying to fill the void in my heart that was left by leaving my father. I was searching for a daddy's love and the long journey led me down Heart Break Road time and time again.

I didn't recognize the real meaning of love therefore I went looking for it in the wrong places. I'm not saying he didn't love me; I just didn't feel it. My view of how love should be, was tainted and stained by being sexually abused as a child by someone I knew. Every encounter I experienced with boys in my teen years, I thought was love. Instead, it turned out to be false promises, lies, and hurt feelings.

My misconception of love led to being used and abused by boys who knew nothing about real love. My father never really understood the damage "lack of affection" caused to his little girl. I hid behind the veil of rejection most of my life; wanting to be accepted by the man who helped give me life; wanting to feel love with common gestures, like a kiss on the cheek or just a simple hug, not just lip service. I would look at my friends interact with their fathers; the smiles, the hugs, the encouragement, the look of "I'm proud to call you my daughter" is what I longed for and always hoped for growing up. My dad would sometimes tell me "you know I love you", but hardly never expressed love outwardly. His reason was he didn't grow up receiving a lot of affection from his parents. It was so hard for him to express something so natural and so needed, only because he didn't know how to. He loved me the way he was taught to love. My dad was very stern, and I realized after I became an adult that this is how he showed love and care for someone.

    No matter how I felt inside, my dad had a killer smile that made my heart melt. I was always happy to see his smile, so disappointing him meant that I let him down and his smile that I so loved so much, disappeared. Doing something wrong often led to lectures for what seemed like hours and Dad would still manage to spank and punish me afterwards. He made me feel as if nothing I did was ever good enough or right for him. I don't remember many times where he told me he was proud of me. There were a few times where he expressed it, but not many. "Black sheep" was how I labeled myself, as if I didn't belong in the family. Deep down in my heart, I knew my dad loved me, but I just didn't feel the love. I often wondered what hindered him from showing me love the way I saw my friends' dad love on them. I know my dad and stepmother were trying to prepare me for the world, but sometimes I just needed a little softness and tenderness from them.

I wish I had known then that God wanted to be my father and give me all the love I was lacking. He wanted to fill the void I had in my heart with His agape love. He wanted to show me what His love was all about, but I didn't recognize His still small voice. All the noise and chaos going off in my mind clogged my spiritual hearing and I missed the call of God in my younger years, causing myself unnecessary suffering and pain for years to come. Knowing what I know now, it was God who I should have opened my heart to. With all the hurt and pain, I went through, I understand God wanted me to open my heart to Him.

Now my mom on the other hand was the total opposite of my dad. Mother and I were very close through my adolescent years and while I were growing up as a teenager. Even though we had our differences, I always knew I could count on her to get me through the growing pains of life no matter how old I was. I was her one and only child and she made sure she showered me with gifts (this was her way of showing love) and told me how beautiful I was every day. People say I was spoiled as a child but, my rebuttal to them is, my mother gave me just a little extra love. Mother has always been the caring and nurturing type. She hugged and kissed me every chance she got. I considered Mother to be a free spirit; loud, boldly stating her opinion with no filters. She helped anyone who she met, not worrying about her own issues or circumstances, but making sure everyone else was ok. Mother would give a stranger the shirt off her back if she had to. Her heart was always giving by taking people in until they got on their feet. She never thought twice about it because she knew where her blessings came from.

On the flip side of things, my mom also dealt with the spirit of suicide. Her inner issues caused her to drink a lot as well. When I was fifteen years old, I remember witnessing Mother's suicide attempt. It makes me emotional just thinking about it. She'd just lost her job, the bills were stacking up, and she didn't know how she was going to provide for us. Mother was sitting in a chair in the living room; and there were various kinds of liquor bottles and pills on the table. She had a huge kitchen knife in one hand, trying to cut her wrist on the other hand. She was staring off in a gaze with tears flowing down her cheeks.

I didn't know what to say to her or how to console her. So, I made a quick decision to call my aunt to see if she could help. My aunt told me to place the phone on speaker and she immediately began to pray. She started praying against that suicide demon as though this was going to be her last spiritual battle against the devil. She knew she was at war with Satan and his army and she did not want to play with him! During the prayer I was able to take the knife out of my mother's hand. She grabbed me and hugged me so tight that I could feel her heart beating super-fast. We both held one another and cried.

I remember thanking God for keeping her from doing what I thought was the inevitable, but part of me was also angry because I didn't understand why God allowed this to happen. It felt as if He wasn't there in the very moment that my mom attempted to take her life; I was numb and couldn't feel His presence. I felt hopeless not being able to help her. Now I understand why my grandfather would always quote this scripture: Fear not; for I am with thee; be not dismayed; for I am thy God: I will strengthen thee; yea I will help thee; yea, I will uphold thee with the right hand of my righteousness (Isaiah 41:10). As I stood there looking at Mother, I was in shock and began to cry harder at the thought of losing her. I'm not sure what I would have done if my mother was successful at taking her life that night, but this scripture instantly brought peace to me.

All my friends loved my mom just as much as I did, but I was too ashamed to tell them what we were going through. I knew they would be crushed to hear such a thing, so I kept it to myself. They also loved to spend the night at my house because they knew Mother was cool and would buy them nice things. I swear I had the most slumber parties growing up! My mom would sit around with us while we talked about boys, hoping to enlighten us on how to be young ladies. Oh, those were the good ole' days! Mother loved seeing me happy and smiling, but it would break her heart when I would cry about the relationship between Dad and me. The comfort she gave would only put a "Band-Aid" over the deep wound in my heart. All I wanted was some tender love and care from my "Superman".

As a teenager, I didn't understand that everything I was going through in life, was helping to make and mold me into who God was calling me to be. My self-esteem was so low from striving to please my parents and from trying to be perfect, I didn't even love myself or think I was beautiful. I was just a pretty face in a crowd waiting on someone to notice me; waiting for someone to remove the mask which hid the pain I was feeling inside...

Nothing but a Pretty Face
I'm nothing but a pretty face full of meekness and grace; just an image for others to see, never realizing there's more to me. Just another pretty face standing in the crowd, screaming "I am somebody," out loud. Is anyone listening to the silent tears I cry? No, they're just staring at me as they walk by. As the tears roll down my "pretty face" cheeks, the Lord whispers in my ear, "stay humble and

sweet; I have you standing there for all to see that I am the one who is blessing you and setting you free! When I am done molding you on my potter's wheel, your future will be sealed; for I am God and through you, my glory shall be revealed."

 All the negative words spoken to me as a child from various people in my life began to fester on the inside causing, a lack of self-love and self-respect. The disdain rejection imprinted a permanent stain in my mind and in my heart. The root of rejection that was planted in me as a child began to grow. I began to think I was unlovable. Not dealing with the spirit of rejection led me down the wrong path and caused me to make many bad decisions.

 My only outlet was playing sports and participating in as many school activities as I could just to keep my mind off my pain. Sports was something I was good at and the joy of participating in sports helped me to escape my inner turmoil. Being the natural athlete that I was, every sport I chose to participate in, I excelled in. My grades were top notch due to my father stressing the importance of staying focused in school. I considered myself to be an over achiever! Basketball, softball, track, and volleyball fueled my drive for perfection. However, there was a negative side that I also latched on to. Drinking and smoking weed to escape the voices which re-played repeatedly in my head about my failures and mistakes, was a temptation that could have been avoided. 1 Corinthians 10:13 says, there hath no temptation taken you, but such as is common to man: but God is faithful, who will not suffer you to be tempted above that ye are able; but will with the temptation also make a way to escape, that ye may be able to bear it. I was often reminded of my past, reminded of how I was a "disappointment and let down." Like many other teens, I felt so misunderstood. The damage was done, the wall around my heart stood firm, built out of concrete; nothing or no one would be able to penetrate this wall of false protection that I created for myself. I was determined that no one was ever getting in to hurt me again.

Psalms 127:3 says, lo, children are a heritage of the Lord: and the fruit of the womb is his reward. Here it was, the Lord gave me to my loving parents as a blessing from Him. Yet they couldn't figure out how to nurture me. They didn't know how to cultivate the gifts and talents God put in me. I don't even think they recognized the call of God that was on my life. If they would have prayed against those negative seeds that were planted in me as a child, those childhood seeds would have never taken root and grown into adult issues and problems. Maybe just maybe, I wouldn't have dealt with low self-esteem or rejection as a child and teenager. Their prayers would have help build my confidence, the kind of confidence which stops you from looking for love in all the wrong places. That confidence which kills out any feelings of thinking I wasn't loved as a child or nothing I did was ever good enough. And to this day, I am still dealing with the seed of rejection, trying to figure out how to uproot it from my life. But this is what I love about the Holy Ghost and this is what makes God who He is: the power of the Holy Ghost allows God to hide the anointing in plain sight. Even though I was constantly reminded of my past and my feelings of being unloved and unwanted, it still didn't stop the call God placed on my life. As you continue to read on you will see how the presence of God became more and more prevalent in my life.

Sharee A. Smith

This So-Called Single Life
Married for 13 years; knew the end was near.
kept crying tears...
Tears of sorrow, tears of tomorrow, tears of pain.
tears of being insane...
Insane in my mind, insane in my heart
wondering if I would ever get a fresh start
Start into a new transition, an attempt to get in position.
But my life was full of opposition!
Opposition from the north, south, east, and west.
it forced me to put in a few requests, to God that is...
Is this single life all that it is cracked up to be?
Is there a penalty for breaking up the family tree?
Are my children's future truly gone or will they ever be able to sing a new song?
Songs of yesterday tells my story.
of how God delivered me through His glory...
Glory that we will never fully understand.
because God made us human and called us "Man"...
Man, my life was so messed up.
God was calling me to come in and sup...
Sup with Him that is, about this thing called I call "single."
I thought I would be free to mingle; free to play; free to lay...

Lay with whomever I so choose;
in the end I would ultimately lose...
Lose my freedom of choice, my spiritual voice;
lose my witness through bodily fitness...
Fitness that doesn't mean a thing; especially if it ain't got that swing!
Swinging into the arms of the devil;
never accepting the call to come up another level;
binding that man's soul up, where he can never be free,
regretting the day, he laid with me...
Is this so-called single life all that it's cracked up to be?
I don't know, you tell me!

Table of Contents

Life Happens 1
My Darling Randy 9
Big Disappointment 17
Doing the Unthinkable 28
Courage to Leave 35
Price of Freedom 48
Bag Lady 58
The Pain Inside 69
Mr. NFL Himself 76
Relationship Blues 84
The Birdman 91
A Change of Heart 101
God's Request 106
Perfect Timing 117
The Courtship 124
New Beginnings 133

Life Happens

(Disclaimer: Please read the Preface, it provides a great understanding about my life and why I told the story the way I did.)

The gavel dropped, and my horrible truth was finally over. I can still smell the ink drying after signing my divorce papers. Ahhh, what a breath of fresh air, I thought, while sitting in the empty courtroom weeping tears of joy. I was so caught up in my moment of glory I didn't even realize everyone except myself had exited the room. I'd just been through the worst period of my life. My divorce was final, and I was free as a kite flying in the wind. Nothing was holding me back. There was a box of Kleenex sitting on the table next to me. I gathered my thoughts, wiped my face, and left the courtroom. As I walked outside, I was careful to take every step and stride in confidence. I got in my car and headed home. While there, I slipped into some relaxing clothes and headed straight to the computer. I needed the dating world to know that I was single and ready to mingle!

As I sat in front of my computer, starring at the black screen, I decided to update my status on "My Space". While waiting for the computer to boot up, the pain and anguish of what I'd been through hit me all at once. All the emotions that come with divorce began to plague my mind. Feelings of anger, defeat, failure, guilt, and regret started to grip my heart. My 13-year plunge into marriage had just gone down the drain, carrying a web of deceit with it.

It was hard for me to accept the fact that the man I married had been so physically and verbally abusive. And that green-eyed ugly monster "Jealousy" had been the culprit to fuel his rage. I hid behind the shadows of this tyrant whom everyone thought was a great man of God, a loyal husband, and the best father to his children they had ever seen. But little did they know, he was the total opposite of what anyone ever imagined, and it even took me by surprise! His betrayal, control, insecurities, manipulation, and unfaithfulness had taken its toll on me. It all left me with feelings of emptiness. I had nothing else left in me to give to the man who was supposed to be my "forever"! Up to that time, he had been my best friend, my lover, and my husband. My mind and heart were left in a state of confusion which made me question my very existence. So, I secluded myself away from family and friends, and wore depression as if it were a coat. The guilt, shame, and sorrow I felt was indescribable and undeniable. Never in a million years would I have ever thought my marriage would end.

In the beginning I saw many signs of abuse but ignored them. Being young and naïve blinded me from what I thought was love. Since I was happy to be a mother and wife, the thought of being married out-weighed the flashing warning signs. My ex-husband shared stories with me about how his family experienced abuse at the hands of his stepfather, not realizing how the abuse really affected him. We met during a time in my life when I didn't have much guidance and turning 18 was the highlight of my life! It was apparent that I didn't know anything about living the adult life I was so longing for. I was looking for love in all the wrong places while trying to discover who I was. In addition to this, my father and stepmother had just put me out of their house with nowhere to go. Thankful my mom had a longtime friend from her military days who allowed me to stay with her.

My ex-husband was someone I thought would allow me to be myself and be free. I thought he would allow me to be imperfect, especially coming from my father's house where it seemed that I had to do everything right. A place where I had to pay for my mistakes. A place where almost everything I did seemed like it was negatively critique. A place where I was talked down upon at times. A place where I had no peace. A place where the words "you know I love you" took the place of hugs and kisses. A place where it felt like I had to pay for the mistakes of my mother. A place of control and a deep-seated unbearable pain. A place where I experienced rejection at its finest. I thought my ex-husband would save me from all the bad I experienced growing up and all the pain I endured through my teenage years. He was supposed to fill the void of emptiness and hopelessness in my heart. I didn't know that God would one day fill that empty space with Himself.

Since family was so important to me, I wouldn't have ever thought my children would come from a broken, dysfunctional home and a product of divorce. I fought so hard to keep my family together, but I just could not take any more abuse, nor could I subject them to what I felt was torment. I thought it was important for him to fight for the marriage, but he refused. It got to the point that my children feared their father, not with a Godly reverence, but with a fear that gripped their hearts for years to come. It came to the point where I had to make a decision that would break up the family, but I knew it was for the best. All evidence pointed to the fact that the violence would continue, and my children and I would suffer unwanted abuse and an expected demise. As a protector of my family, I knew we deserved better.

As I started the journey of being a single parent, I had to make decisions for the betterment of my three children. There was my oldest, Destiny, who was the momma's girl and kept me close to her heart. She valued her time with me. Destiny always tried to stay out of trouble, and was a very sweet, loving, and helpful daughter. She prided herself with spending time with her siblings whenever I was at work or running errands. Our daughter carried a lot of responsibilities on her shoulders while we were a family.

Faith, my middle child, was the ray of sunshine in the family. Her smile illuminated the room. I called her my artistic child because she loved to draw, write songs and poetry, sing, and listen to music. She's been gifted to play the violin and keyboard by never having taken lessons. She always thought differently from her siblings. And we called her "out little genius" because she was always thinking outside of the box. However, there was a rebellious side of her, in which, she would throw tantrums when she could not have her way. She was a daddy's girl at heart and was always crying for her daddy even after the divorce.

Finally, there was my baby boy Winston who he served as the peacemaker of the family. He too was a momma's boy at heart but thought he was the man of the house. He was very mild mannered most of the time and loved to crack jokes on his sisters. He enjoyed playing video games and football. Winston was quite the lady's man and loved to charm women at a young age. I didn't have any problems from him as a child. He did his best to stay out of trouble and to make good decisions growing up as a young black child and young black male in this society.

Most of the time the kids got along well, however, there were times where sibling rivalry would arise. One example was the time when the girls got into a physical altercation. I decided to teach them a lesson ace wrapping their wrist and legs together. They had to work as one to move together. This forced them to realize that they needed each other in order to accomplish the goal of getting along. I did not like my kids fighting because I did not want them to grow up thinking this was how families were supposed to deal with conflict. We endured enough violence while I was married to their dad.

I did not wait to feel sorry for myself, instead I had to pick up the pieces and move on. It was as if a door opened and I was now a single parent raising three children alone in this dark, crazy, hopeless world. I was not sure if I was equipped to be able to do such an enormous job on my own. The thought and responsibility of raising three kids by myself was terrifying. I was left alone to worry about the emotional and mental state of three innocent little people and all their needs including daycare, extracurricular activities, before and after school care, and doctor visits, etc. I was left alone to pick up the pieces of our shattered lives. It was hard for me to look them in their eyes and explain to them that I and their father had divorced. They were so young, and I knew they would not really understand the reasons why I decided to leave. How do you explain adult decisions to small children? How do you put into words all the hurt, pain, and guilt I felt without bashing the man my youngest daughter deemed her "Super-Superman"?

I began to question myself about how could I have allowed Satan to rip my family apart? All these thoughts captured my mind and heart. Could we have fasted and prayed more? Could we have gone to more counseling sessions? Could we have prayed more together as a family? Could I have been more patient? What could I have done differently to fix my perplexed marriage? It had gotten so bad, that I was ready to give up on life. I could not and would not suffer any longer. I said I trusted God to repair the damage, but did I really trust that God is sovereign, and He could do anything? I just wanted out! I could not and would not suffer another day! I wanted to escape the blame, the drinking, the infidelity, mental, physical, verbal abuse, and the unstableness. I felt like a caged bird who wanted to be free but couldn't fly because my wings were broken! I was the caterpillar in the cocoon who was going through a metamorphosis; waiting on God to make me into a beautiful butterfly with beautiful colors in my wings which to me, represented freedom, joy, happiness, and security! I wanted to break through my shell and fly! It made me realize that if I didn't make a change soon, my children would end up with a shattered life, possibly without their mother and I couldn't do that to them.

People thought we had a perfect life and a perfect marriage. Why, because I covered him so well. To them, we were a perfect couple. We loved taking photos together, but the family portraits painted a picture of illusion. Brokenness and defeat were hidden behind our smiles that displayed happiness and togetherness. You know the saying "a picture is worth a thousand words?" Well, those family photos sold the American dream to many people who saw them. When you saw him, you saw me. We were like a set of twins, inseparable; two peas in a pod! We did most things together as a family. Figuratively speaking, this man was the lace to my shoes, the glue to my wall paper, the peanut butter to my jelly, you get the picture! We were a match made in heaven, so people thought, so, I thought.

My Darling Randy

The lust of the flesh, the lust of the eyes, and the pride of life is a sure way to separate yourself from God and all the many blessings He has in store for you. These things will have you trying to fill a void only God can fill. Lust is so deceiving that it led me down many wrong paths in life, paths that could have been avoided. If I'd only gotten a hold on the Word of God at an early age, it would helped have me stay focus on the things of God...

My mother's friend and her daughter invited me to a party one night that would open the door and set me on a course for a real-life experience. The story I'm about to tell you is about my first love named Randy and the intricate part he played in my truth. He was the first friend I met in L.A. He went to Jefferson High School, where he was a member of the boys' varsity basketball team. He lived downtown with his father and little brother and like most single parents with children I knew, stayed in a 2-bedroom apartment. I don't remember much about his mom, except that she didn't live with them. She had her own place not too far from where they stayed. How would I have ever known that this invitation would lead me to a young man that would impact part of my destiny, my story?

There he was, standing by the DJ booth staring at me, tall, brown-skinned and looking so fine! Of course, I decided to play the shy role and act like I wasn't checking him out in his Levi jeans, unbuttoned plaid shirt, with a tucked in white tee shirt, with white tennis shoes on. We locked eyes as I attempted to look away. He quickly made his way over to the side of the room where I was standing to ask me to dance with him. "The way she shakes her bootay sho' look good to me", he was singing some of the words to the song as he grabbed my hand and pulled me to the dance floor. While we were dancing, he tried to make small talk. We both found ourselves yelling over the loud music just to hear one another! I turned around and made a suggestive move according to the song. This let him know just how interested I was. So, he grabbed my waist and we continued to dance until the song went off. We decided to go outside on the balcony to enjoy the nice, cool breeze. We were both drenched in sweat from all that booty shaking!

He introduced himself as Randy and begun to tell me how he couldn't help but notice me as I walked through the door with my friend. We were dressed alike wearing the latest clothing trends, knowing we would turn heads! Looking around, he expressed that he thought he would be the only teenager at his father's party. But when he saw me coming through the door, he knew his night would be cool. As a young girl in my day would say, he had me cheesin' from ear to ear, even though I was trying to play the shy role! So, I reached out to shake his hand and told him my name. Meeting new people was not my forte, but the way he came at me broke the ice! And yeah, I was checking him out too with that school girl gleam in my eyes, the look you give when you are crushing on someone. I cannot tell a lie, he was looking good; tall and slim just like I liked them! He ended up being my dancing partner for the rest of the night.

Later, during the evening, our conversations led from talking about one thing to the other. He wanted to know what made me come to L.A. I explained to him that this was not my first time living in Los Angeles. I also lived in there as a young child when my mom was in the military. Once she got out of the military she decided to remain in Los Angeles and I moved back St. Louis to live with my father. While there I completed middle school and afterwards, we moved to Georgia, where I completed one year of high school. After that, I came back to L.A. to be with my mother.

I found myself expounding about how I got many different opportunities to travel the states because my mom was in the armed services and was stationed in Seoul, Korea for three years while I was in elementary school. I wanted to live with her so badly, but my dad would not allow it. He didn't want me to live out because it would have been harder for him to see me during this time. Man, did I miss my mom when she was gone. We talked almost every day! She would send big huge boxes full of clothes and shoes from Korea just for me, jackets and shoes that no one else had. I remember her sending me this red leather "Beat It" jacket with exactly 32 zippers. And you know I counted each one of them! It looked just like the one Michael Jackson had in the "Beat It" video. I was the only one in my school who had one! I became a trend setter in elementary school with fancy clothes and leather jackets. I loved getting boxes from her and they were always full of surprises. I would come home from school and there the big box was, sitting in the middle of the floor in the living room addressed to "Sherry", not the name on my birth certificate, but the name everyone in my family calls me even to this day! I couldn't believe I'd just shared my life story with him, lol! I usually don't do this when I first meet someone, but he made me feel that I could be open and honest with him and that whatever I told him would be kept between us.

Meeting Randy for the first time was very impressionable and well worth it. He sure did know how to charm a lady! He was polite and handsome. He had a small overbite and nice white teeth. And his smile, honey let me tell you, was worth a million dollars! He won me over with his charm and personality. How could I say no to him! My school girl crush became more than a crush. It became an infatuation with a boy I barely knew. I had a good feeling about Randy and it seemed that things would be promising with us.

As we stood on the balcony and talked for what seemed like hours, the DJ began to play another one of my favorite songs, but this time it was one of my favorite slow jams. I was surely hoping Randy would ask me to dance again. Right as the thought crossed my mind, he grabbed me and pulled me closer to him. He placed my arms around his neck and his hands around my waist and we began to slow dance right there on the balcony. Chills went up and down my back! His chest was warm and firm, which represented strength, and meant that I could lean on him when I needed him. I could feel his heart beating extremely fast as my head lay there. I thought to myself, "Dang, I guess he knows what he wants, or he is just really excited to be here, in this moment with me."

His boldness and aggression turned me on. He held me so tight and close that I didn't want him to let me go. All these thoughts were racing through my mind about him asking me to be his girl. How could this be from someone so young? At that instance he made me feel protected, like I belonged in his arms. He made me feel very comfortable. I felt secure with him. Even though his heart was beating fast from nervousness as if he didn't know what my reaction was going to be, he continued to hold on to me. That gesture was the beginning of something special. I did not want the moment to end, nor that night. The reality of it all was that the song was only about four minutes long. But that four minutes seemed like an eternity! Well, at least that's what I wanted it to be! The song finally ended, and our first slow dance was over.

We both stood there in silence, wondering what to say. That moment was very awkward. I looked at him and went in for the kiss! Instantly, I thought that he would turn his head, but he didn't. It turned out that he wanted to kiss me as badly as I wanted to kiss him. It was the sweetest, most sensual kiss I've ever experienced. He must have known in that moment that the time was right for him to seal the deal. We both stood there in the same awkward silence from before, with peculiar looks on our faces. So many thoughts were going through my mind while we were kissing. I wasn't sure if he would like it or if he thought I was moving too fast. His lips looked so tasty and the way he kept on licking them, made me curious about what would happen next. The mood was set after that slow dance. The way he was holding me completely turned me on and I felt his manhood bulging through his jeans!

When we finally snapped out of the trance, we realized the party was coming to an end and people were starting to leave. I was glad we got a chance to meet. He wrote my number down in his hand, guaranteeing me that he would not forget it. I reminded him to keep in touch with me as he softly rubbed his hand across my cheek. We stepped back into what was left of the party to say our "goodbyes". He walked me to the door, gave me a hug and a kiss on the cheek, and closed the door as I walked out. All I thought about the whole car ride home was that daunting kiss! He really captured my attention. Once I got home and found that mom was sound asleep, I took a shower and went to sleep thinking about Randy. Our night together had me intrigued and wanting more of his company. I just couldn't shake him! Although I wasn't sure when he would call but I anxiously waited. He had me so mesmerized, that I completely forgot to get his number. So, I had no choice but to wait on a call from him. The night ended on a very good note and with Randy in mind, I dozed right off to sleep.

Randy delivered on his word regarding our first date about a week after we met. We started hanging out more frequently. Our new-found friendship developed into something greater than just being friends. We shared mutual feelings for one another, so much, that we began dating shortly after we met. We did everything together and I mean everything! We hung out at the beach, movies, school dances, his apartment, and my apartment. He would go places with my mom and me. We would often play basketball against each other, since we both loved sports. He was a Center and I was a Forward. We both were competitive, but I knew he would let me win sometimes simply because he was taller than me! Sometimes he would even come visit me at my school. It seemed like we could not be kept apart! Randy met all my close friends that I hung out with and I met all his close friends. His father loved me, and my mother loved Randy. Who knew our relationship would last for two years?

I remember my first sexual encounter with Randy. It happened about two weeks after we started dating. I was home from school that day because of a Teacher's Workday. He decided to skip school, so that we could spend the whole day together. While on the phone the night before, we made plans for him to come over. My mom had to work both of her jobs, so that meant that I would be home alone all day! Early the next morning, he rode the bus from his school and came to my house. It took him what seemed like forever to get to my house. In the meantime, I made sure I had showered, cleaned my room, and even cooked us some breakfast. Since we had no way to contact each other except through pay phone, I made him promise that he would call me as soon as he got off the bus near my house. I was excited and nervous the entire time waiting for him. The feel of fluttering butterflies left a nauseous feeling in my stomach. Since my apartment complex was about two blocks from the bus stop, I decided to meet him halfway. So, I sat anxiously by the phone waiting for it to ring. Finally, the phone rung and it was him.

I was super excited to hear his voice and the anticipation showed on my face. He made me feel so good inside! He'd just gotten off the bus in front of the 7-Eleven and was calling to see if I wanted anything from the store. I let him know that I didn't want anything but was headed out to meet him. I tossed and turned all night waiting for this day to come. Now the moment is finally here! I became a little impatient while waiting for him to exit the store. I wondered in my mind just why he needed to stop by the store anyways! I put on my shoes and we both hung up the phone.

(He never mentioned that the real reason he stopped by the store was to purchase condoms).

I ran down the stairs and out of the door as fast as I could. As I was turning the corner of my apartment complex, I saw Randy off in the distance. Man was I walking fast. We ran up to each other at the halfway point. He hugged me, he picked me up off my feet, and swung me around in a circle, planting a huge kiss on my cheek. We turned around and headed back to my house. Along the way, we talked about his interminable bus ride and about how he fell asleep half way through the ride, almost missing the stop by my house. All I could do was laugh! We finally arrived to my house, I unlocked the door, and Randy followed me in. After I closed the door, Randy turned around and began to kiss me passionately. I couldn't resist as I placed my arms around his neck. They rested comfortably on his shoulders as our bodies pushed against the door. I gently pulled away from him and guided him over to the kitchen table so that we could eat the breakfast that I'd prepared earlier that morning for us; eggs, bacon, and toast. I turned on the television to see what was on but had no clue of what to watch because under normal circumstances, I am usually at school during this time of the day. My nervous jitters made me lose my appetite, so I tried to make small conversation to take the attention off my nervousness.

We talked about the football game I wanted him to accompany me to on Friday night. I really wanted him to come to the game with me because I didn't have many friends yet. I kept looking down at my un-eaten food, trying not to make eye contact with him. I sensed he would see the nervous fear through my eyes. He stretched his hand out to touch my face. As he caressed the side of my cheek, he asked why I was looking down at my plate. I didn't know how to answer that question, however, I knew that we were about to have sex for the first time and I was afraid and nervous. I thought I was going to pass out because, with this being my first time, I wasn't sure if he would be pleased with me. I had no sexual experience whatsoever, but he promised he would be gentle with me as he leaned over to kiss me again. We got up from the table and headed upstairs to my room, leaving behind my plate of uneaten food. My hands were trembling as I led him to my room. We closed the door behind us.

Big Disappointment

We may not ever fully understand why we must go through certain things in our lives, but it's through God that we find this understanding. It's through Him we find our peace in the midst of the storm. Because I was as young as I was, I confused lust with love. I still say, due to the absence of my dad and the lack of affection, I didn't know how to love myself. So, I got caught up during a time when I should have been trying to mend the relationship with my dad. Being stiff-necked and hardheaded caused me to endure one of the hardest situations I ever had to face in life...

As time progressed, my relationship with Randy grew stronger. I'd never been more committed to anything or anyone else in my life. My first experience of what I cherished as true love meant a lot to me. Along with our blossoming relationship, there was school, and my life at home. My mother expected me to be involved in every school activity there was! She said that staying busy would keep me out of trouble. She would always ask me about school, but her main concern was why it always took me so long to get home in the evening. She felt that since we stayed directly behind the school, it shouldn't have taken me that long to get home.

It had been 6 months since I started my new school. Mother swore that I should be well adjusted and making new friends by now. My answer to her was always the same..."School is school, nothing new." I did try out for the basketball team that day but didn't want to tell her. I didn't want her to be disappointed if I had not been selected to be on the team. We wouldn't find out for another week if we'd made the team or not. She expressed her concern regarding the tiredness in my voice. I'd just gotten home from a long, grueling school day, including after-school tryouts. My entire body was aching and all I wanted to do lay down.

She kept looking at me intensely and I assumed it was because I was purposely ignoring her questions. I was exhausted and didn't want to have any conversations about school. So, I promised that I would talk about later. After running the bleachers and up and down the basketball court, my weary feet needed some immediate rest! As I headed up the steps to my room, Mother yelled from the kitchen that she would wake me up when dinner was ready.

As I entered the bedroom door, I placed my book bag next to the bed, kicked off my shoes, and stretched out across my bed. I heard Mom screaming for me to take a shower, but I was just was not up to it. My whole body was hurting, so my desire was to lie still for a while and get some much-needed rest. It occurred to me that I had not played any sports since middle school. Basketball tryouts enlightened me to the fact that I was completely out of shape and out of sync with conditioning my body!

Before I knew it, I had dozed off into a deep sleep. I remember dreaming about running up and down that basketball court, bouncing the ball real fast as my coach was chasing me. It seemed that I was trying to get away but did not see an exit door! Coach told us that if he caught up with us, we would not make the team. I was so frightened by my Coach's announcement, that the ball hit my foot and went left into my teammate's way. As I went after the ball, my teammate and I collided and fell! That is when I suddenly woke up out of the dream, sweating and breathing hard, wondering in my mind if the dream had any significant meaning to me making the team. Oh well, I couldn't worry about it now because I would find out next week. No worries though on my part! I had skills when it came to basketball, along with volleyball, softball, and track. I got up off the bed, grabbed my clothes, and rushed down the hall to the bathroom to take a shower. Mom was on her way up the stairs, which is what woke me up from that horrid dream of mine!

She wanted to let me know that dinner was ready, and she wanted us to eat together. Mother still wanted to know how I was adjusting to my new environment at school and if I was making any new friends. I hope she made my favorite meal: fried chicken, mac-n-cheese, yams, and collard greens! With it being a weekday, I doubt it. She probably made her favorite food, tacos! I swear we ate tacos at least three times a week. I finished up in the shower and hurried downstairs to eat. To my surprise, she'd made meatloaf, mashed potatoes, and cabbage, my second favorite dinner!

As I sat down to the table and began scarfing my food down, my mom slapped the fork out of my hand because I started eating without saying grace. I was very hungry and couldn't believe that I made it through tryouts without having any food or energy! While we ate dinner, I told Mother I was thinking about joining Student Council. I learned the importance of staying involved at school at an early age and I wanted to make sure my name was known in a good way with my teachers and peers. We also talked about basketball tryouts which meant I didn't have to explain why I was so sluggish earlier when I came in from school. She fussed at me for not eating lunch when I knew I had tryouts. She also fussed about how I could have passed out from not eating. "When you make the team, you can't be skipping out on lunch, you need energy for practice." Her voice began to fade as I tuned her out.

I assured her I would eat tomorrow for the second day of tryouts. I informed her that the Student Council Information meeting would be held after tryouts for anyone interested in joining for the upcoming school year. So, I would be later than usual getting home. I hated when my mom nagged me about school. I quickly changed the subject and asked her how her day went at work. She began to explain to me how her boss had her working on a special project that had to be completed by the end of her workday. Other than that, she said her day was cool. Mother was glad to hear I was getting involved in school because it would keep me out of mischief, and it would also make the school year go by faster.

I smiled and continued eating my food. One of Mom's rules was for me to clean up the kitchen after she cooked. I swear I hated washing dishes. We had a dishwasher, but she never allowed me to use it. She always said it used too much water and using it would make me lazy. I wondered what was the purpose having a dishwasher if I couldn't use it! After dinner, Mom retreated to her room and I went to the living room to watch television. I always had tons of homework due to my exhausting schedule. Since my time was so limited, it was always a privilege and pleasure when I could watch television. Thank God, I'd finished all my homework before tryouts, so my night was free to do whatever I wanted to do!

As I watched television I began to think about life at school. Over the past 6 months, I adjusted well to my new environment. I'd made plenty of friends and became very popular. My school was heavily populated with over 1,600 students. We were a multicultural school with Hispanics and Latinos making up a majority of the population. Of course, we had the different clicks just like every other school throughout the USA. The weirdo's, the jocks, the nerds, the preppy kids, the gangs, etc. Whatever people had in common with someone is who they hung out with. I mostly hung around the jocks and cheerleaders because of my love for sports. And they appeared to have the most fun!

My school had an area called the Quad where my friends and I would meet up for lunch. Since we had an hour to spare, we would sometimes go off campus to eat. School lunch was fine, but not something I wanted to eat every day. Also, there was a concession stand that served a variety of foods that could be purchased daily. My favorite thing to buy was the MARTINELLI's Apple Juice in the little glass jar shaped like an apple. They only cost fifty cents and I would drink two each day! We had some of the best pep rallies on the Quad during the fall and spring months! There was a DJ, music, dancing, and cheering the football and basketball team on to victory. We also had school dances every Friday night after every home football game. Man, the school dances were so much fun! I used to dance battle Alexis and her twin sister Artesia; they swore they could beat me dancing! Those were definitely some of the best times!

Since I was an only child, my mom would always allow friends to spend weekends with me, especially on my birthday. She often ease-dropped when we talked about what was going on at school. That was really her way of hearing us gossip about the boys. My friends loved Mother and considered her to be the hippest mom they knew! It seemed like she never met a stranger and treated my friends' parents as if she had been knowing them forever. When we went shopping, she would not only buy things for me, but for them too! I remember once when we stayed in Inglewood, we lived upstairs from a lady with five kids. Mom and the lady became very good friends and she would sometimes babysit me when Mom went out. One of the lady's daughters and I became close friends. We were like sisters and because of this, Mom would take her school shopping and buy us matching outfits!

Living with a single mom had its pros and cons. One of the worst cons during this time was not having my father around. I lived in California and he lived in Georgia. We talked on the phone sometimes, but not often. When I would call, he wouldn't want to always get on the phone. So, I would end up talking to my stepmother instead. As a teenager, Dad and I did not have an emotional connection. My mom had male friends I could have talked to and bonded with, however, it would not have been the same as having my father's love and bonding with him. Another con was that my mom wasn't always home, which meant I had a lot unsupervised time alone. I didn't get in trouble with the law, however, I was doing things I had no business doing at my age. My house would be the place where Randy would come to whenever we needed intimacy. We were never intimate at his house because someone was always there.

Mom and I went through some rough times when I were a teenager. Even though we experienced a lot of hardship, my mom did not live off the system. She simply did what she had to do to survive. We really needed my dad's financial support, but from what I was told by Mother, we never received it. Lack of supervision allowed me to have company whenever I wanted to. I skipped school a lot to be with Randy and my friends. We would have frequent parties with my friends. I must give myself some props, even though I skipped a lot of school, I was still able to maintain my grades. I was an A/B Honor Roll student athlete. My teachers loved me and I loved them! I also loved being an only child because my mom bought me whatever I wanted, whenever I wanted it! She hated to see me crying and pouting when I couldn't have my way.

Even though I was busy with school life and all the activities I was involved in, I still found time to spend time with Randy. About a year and a half into our relationship, I got pregnant. Never thought this would happen to me. I was 1sixteen years old and was not ready to handle the responsibility of taking care of a baby. I was just a baby myself. While Mother was working two jobs trying to make ends meet, I was secretly being grown.

Randy and I stopped using condoms about a month after we became intimate; and because we were not responsible, the inevitable happened. Being naïve, I trusted him when he assured me that the "pull out" method would work. After the absence of my period for the second month in a row, I knew something was wrong but didn't know what to do about it. I was so afraid to tell Mother about missing my period twice. As time went on, I kept gaining uncontrollable weight, feeling abnormal on the inside and outside, but did not know at that time that I was pregnant. I was sleeping as though I worked two jobs and had the weirdest food cravings ever! My body had changed and felt strange. Although my breast was never small, I'd never seen them as large as they were! And that was the first thing Mother noticed!

One day as I was coming out of the bathroom, she noticed and inquired about the size of my breast. She swore I was pregnant. So, I just was standing there with this dumb founded look on my face. I didn't know if I should respond or just keep quiet. I wondered how in the world she came to that conclusion just by looking at me. Surely, she had some magic powers or something I didn't know about. I was scared out of my mind, looking at the anger in her eyes as she glared at me with disappointment. The tears began to roll down my face when I realized how disappointed she was with me, along with all the other emotions that come with finding out your teenage daughter is pregnant. Even though I had had not took a pregnancy test, I knew I was.

Suddenly she began to yell at me, saying "how could you let this happen?" She let me know that she really trusted me to be responsible. In all fairness, she never knew I was sexually active. Even in this most tense moment, she asked an obvious question, "is it Randy's baby?" I just stood there and looked at her as if she already knew the answer to that question. In my mind I'm thinking she knew it was his baby, so why in the world would she ask me such a stupid question like that! Before I could even answer her she told me it didn't matter because I was too young to have a baby and I wasn't keeping it! She went on and on, ranting about how she couldn't afford to take care of this baby because she could barely take care of us! She cried, screamed, and yelled for the rest of the day.

I tried to apologize to, her but she was not having it! Tears of disappointment and shame streamed down my face. I was so upset with myself and ashamed that I couldn't even look my mom in her face. She turned her back and stormed away from me. I ran in my room and locked the door for fear of her coming into my room. I'd never seen Mother so angry before. All sort of things were going through my mind. Why would she say I couldn't keep the baby? I thought it was my decision. I felt like it was unfair for her to make the decision for me! She didn't even give me a chance to ponder on it or to make sense of it all. As far as she knew, there would be no baby and that was final! I'd hope she would she change her mind about keeping the baby.

In all honestly, I thought she would be happy to have a grandchild, but then the reality hit me! What was I thinking? How could the star student and great athlete get pregnant at sixteen? This situation stirred up feelings of melancholy, and my mind immediately went back to how I longed for a relationship with Dad, and the rejection I experienced growing up. It reminded me of how I felt unloved and unwanted as a child by people I knew. I began to sob even harder, realizing, I'd looked for love in all the wrong places. The feeling of wanting to be accepted and loved all came down to me getting pregnant as a teenager. My mom and I never talked about sex. It was shunned upon as if it wasn't a normal and natural act of affection between two people who loved each other. Mother acted as if I wasn't supposed to think about it. I don't know if she was embarrassed to talk to me about sex or if she just didn't care about it. Everything I learned about sex came from conversations I'd had with my friends and with Randy.

Mom didn't talk to me for days. I didn't know how to react or respond to this, so I made sure I stayed out of her way. I didn't know if she was thinking of how to handle the situation or if she was just that angry with me. After three days of not talking to me, I learned that mom had decided to take me to the military base clinic to get a pregnancy test. We rode in the car in silence, as I stared out of the window. We pulled up to the base clinic and went inside.

Since I was a minor, Mom had to fill out paperwork for the pregnancy test. I just sat quietly with my head down. We waited for hours to be escorted to the examination room. Minors were not allowed to be in the exam room alone, so Mother had to come with me. He told me to have a seat on the patient bed. Mother sat in the empty chair by the door as the doctor began to explain the testing procedures. I had to give a urine sample and take a blood test. If the results came back positive, I would have to have an ultrasound to see how far along I was.

The doctor gave me a cup and I headed down the hall to the restroom. As I closed the door, I could hear my mom and the doctor talking about the situation. Later, I came back in the room where my mom and the doctor were and sat on the bed. By this time the nurse came in to draw my blood. Man, I hated needles and shots. I cringed when I saw how long the needle was. However, the nurse made it a pleasant experience by gently and carefully drawing the blood. When she was done, she disposed of the used needle, gathered the sample, and existed the room without saying a word. What did this mean? I couldn't quiet my thoughts. She made sure to close the door behind her as she was leaving out.

My mom stepped out of the room to make a phone call. Finally, alone in the room, I began to weep. The thought of me getting rid of my baby was very painful. I laid back on the bed and closed my eyes as I waited for the doctor to come in the room. Loudly, I heard footsteps coming up the hallway. As I sat up on the bed, the doctor began to read the results of the pregnancy test. My heart dropped as he said the words "your pregnancy test came back positive." I jumped off the bed and ran out of the room to the bathroom. I locked the door behind me and cried like a little baby that lost her favorite toy.

All I could think about is Mother and her statement to me regarding not keeping the baby, so there was no point in getting an ultrasound. I couldn't bear the thought of hearing the heartbeat of the life growing inside me. Mom knew that if I heard the baby's heartbeat, she would have had a battle on her hands. I gathered myself together, washed my face, and headed back to the room. In the back of my mind, I knew I didn't need a baby. Honestly, I wasn't even sure if I really wanted a baby, but at the same time, I couldn't phantom the thought of aborting my baby.

Doing the Unthinkable

I heard many abortion horror stories from people I knew. Stories of how the doctor uses a vacuum pump to suck the baby out of your womb and the sounds you hear while you are heavily sedated during the procedure. I remembered reading a story in a women's health magazine of a young teenage girl who had an abortion when she was just 15 years old and 3 months pregnant. Her story had me really shook and I knew at that moment I didn't want an abortion. I never got the opportunity to find out how far along I was because I never got the ultrasound. Mother insisted on not knowing since I wasn't keeping the baby.

We left the military base clinic and headed home. We both were quiet the whole ride home with no music playing; just total silence. I was devastated at the thought of having the life that was growing inside of me, ripped to pieces and torn from my body, hurt me to my core! And the fact that this chapter in my life would soon come to an end, hurt even more. Words could not began to describe how I was feeling inside. No baby, no baby shower, no baby names, no baby room, no baby food, no baby clothes, no picking out a crib................ the silent tears began to flow down my cheeks as we rode down the highway. My head was turned towards the window as I stared aimlessly into the clouds. The day was kind of overcast with no sun in sight. My spirit was broken and I was very angry! For the first time in a while I just didn't know what to do. My mom knew what was wrong with me. She didn't even bother to ask me if I was OK. I figured she didn't care anyway because she didn't want me to keep my baby!

I had to apply for government medical assistance because we didn't have money to pay for an abortion. The longer it took for social services to make a decision on granting me medical insurance, the more I grew attached to the little soul growing inside of me. I would lay in my bed at night and wonder if the baby was a boy or girl, how my baby would look, and what color the eyes and hair were. One night, I even dreamt of having a girl. In the dream, she looked just like me. She had long, curly hair and brown eyes and looked to be of toddler age. She was simply beautiful! A dream that will never come true because of the decision my mom made without taking my feelings and thoughts into consideration! It took about a month for us to finally get an approval letter from the social services department, which meant getting an abortion had finally become a reality. As soon as my mom read the letter with my medical information on it, she called the abortion clinic and made my appointment.

The pregnancy and now having to plan to abort this little innocent baby brought about so many emotions. I didn't know how I would break the bad news to Randy. He was so excited when he found out that we conceived. I knew telling him that Mother was making me get rid of his baby was going to be devastating for him as well. You are probably wondering why I didn't stand up to my mother. Well, I was only sixteen years old and I depended on her for everything I ever needed in life. When my mom made up her mind about something, she meant it. She pressured me so bad that I didn't have any mental strength to go against her orders. Arguing with her about it led to nowhere! She even told Randy he would have to go to the abortion clinic with us. I remember talking to him on the phone a few hours before our baby's appointment with death. He pleaded with me not to go through with the abortion. I'd never heard him cry before and I could hear the pain and agony in his voice. He repeated over and over how it was his baby too and that we did not make the decision together. He kept asking me not to kill his baby. It hurt so bad to hear the desperation in his voice that I couldn't even utter out the words to comfort him. He gathered himself together enough to let me know he would meet me at the clinic. He was so disgusted with me that he hung up the phone on me.

My Godmother tagged along for moral support that day. She tried her best to comfort me, telling me Mother meant well. How did she mean well making me kill my unborn child? I just didn't understand! I was so angry at her! I didn't know if I would be able to forgive myself for going through with this act or if I would be able to forgive her for making the decision for me. We arrived at the clinic and Randy was standing outside. You could tell he'd been crying because his eyes were red and swollen. I couldn't even look him in the face. I felt horrible that Mother made him go through this with me. Part of me was glad he was there because I felt that I could have not done it alone.

As we walked through the clinic doors, everyone was quiet. Randy and my Godmother sat down in the waiting area while Mother and I went to the counter to check in. Once we were done, I sat down in the corner chair of the waiting room until they called my name. So many thoughts were racing through my mind, thoughts of my mom's reaction if I changed my mind, thoughts of the procedure and not knowing how it would go, and thoughts of the uncertainty of the future of me and Randy's relationship.

Fifteen minutes later, the nurse called my name and Mother and I headed back to the triage area. While in the triage area, the nurse prepped me for the procedure and told us what to expect during and afterwards. She explained that the process would only take about twenty minutes. My palms began to sweat from nervousness while she continued to talk. She gave me a gown and instructed me to go and change. I had to take off all my clothes, including my underwear and place them in a bag she provided. She also told me to leave the bag there because I would use the same room afterwards for recovery. I got changed and went back to the triage area. I made no eye contact with Mother. As she covered my head with the surgical cap I burst into tears; I couldn't hold them in anymore. She grabbed my hand to comfort me as she walked me to the room where they would perform the procedure.

The room was so cold it caused me to shiver. The doctor instructed me to get on the bed and place my feet into the stirrups. I laid back on the bed and the nurse placed the oxygen mask over my face. As I drifted into a deep sedation from whatever drugs the nurse injected into my I.V., I could hear the doctor counting down as he turned on the machine. I remember faintly hearing the suction of the machine right before I completely went out. After the procedure, I woke up crying because I knew my baby was gone and the pain, I felt in my heart was unbearable. The anesthesia had me vomiting profusely. The heavy bleeding reminded me of the bad periods I had before the pregnancy.

The nurse took me to the recovery room where I was able to relax until I felt well enough to go home. Randy was there waiting on me, still not saying much. I wasn't up for much talking either. We sat there in total silence for about an hour. He helped me put my clothes back on and we went back out into the waiting area. Mother signed all the paperwork while the procedure was being done, so there was nothing else left to do but go home. My

Godmother decided it would be a good idea to get something to eat since it was still early. They took us to the Pancake House, one of our favorite spots. I didn't have much of an appetite, so they ordered my food to go. While we were sitting at the table waiting on the food to come out, Randy expressed his feelings regarding the abortion, with tears and anger. Mother was trying to be understanding but her words just didn't come out right. Randy was so enraged that he got up from the table and ran outside. We packed up his untouched plate of food, paid the waitress, and left. He and Mother argued the entire way to his house. We dropped him off at his apartment and went home. I tried to call and talk to Randy for about a week straight after this but he never answered the phone. He completely ignored all my calls. When he was finally ready to talk, he called me. He stated he was breaking up with me because I killed his baby and that he hated me for it. I was so overwhelmed by his choice of words that I immediately hung up. That was the last time we talked.

Life Lesson

Going through with the abortion traumatized me for years to come. My emotional state was a wreck. I didn't talk to my mom for almost a month. I fell into a slight depression after the abortion. I had feelings of regret and sadness. It was very difficult for me to forgive myself. I knew abortions were a sin in the eyesight of God. The enemy had my mind in a state of confusion. I wanted to blame God and everyone else for this situation I'd gotten myself into. I began to rebel against my mother and God. I didn't realize the dangerous place I was putting myself in. Anger took root and harbored in my heart towards God. I tuned out that still small voice (God) that used to comfort me as a child. God will use what we think is the worst situation in our lives to teach us lessons. God wanted me to remember that this experience didn't change the nature of who He was or His love for me. He was the same person from the bible who my grandmother would read to me about when I was a small child. This experience made me realize I was a survivor and I survived something I'd never gone through before. I probably wouldn't have survived it if God wasn't present, even though I hadn't fully grasped who He was and what role He played in my life during that time. God was trying to teach me He was in control and He just needed me to trust Him. Trusting Him is something I learned later in life through the many test and trials He took me through while being married to my kids' father.

Courage to Leave

No one gets married to get a divorce. You stand before God and all your family and friends and take your vows: "I,____, take thee,____, to be my wedded husband/wife, to have and to hold, from this day forward, for better, for worse, for richer, for poorer, in sickness and in health, to love and to cherish, till death do us part, according to God's holy ordinance; and thereto I pledge thee my faith [or] pledge myself to you." You willingly take this oath not knowing what lies ahead. Two souls become one and from that moment forth you are supposed to be bound together forever. Well at least that's what I thought...

Now, back to talking about the dissolution of my marriage. There were many times where I wanted to leave but never had the courage to do so. I was full of fear and lacked the faith I needed to push forward. I lost my identity in trying to build my ex-husband up. I lived in his shadows, always putting my dreams and desires on the back burner. My world was all about him, including his baggage and mine. The warning signs revealed themselves before we were married but I chose to ignore them. I was so infatuated by the illusion of the man my ex-husband presented himself to be, that I missed the reality of the boy he really was. Lust blinded me and painted a semblance of real love. I didn't know how it was supposed to feel or what it was supposed to personify. It was supposed to exemplify a fondness for someone, and it was supposed to be tender and endearing. Love was supposed to be warm and intimate; not puffed up and selfish. If I only had God's guidance when I met him. I don't recall hearing any still small voice telling me about what lied ahead of me. Where was God? I would always ask myself this question, not knowing that He was there all along.

While working at Bio-Lab, I encountered this couple who were God-fearing church goers. They would talk about the Lord every single day and invited me to come to church with them. They wore me down talking about the things of God! One day I finally accepted their offer and decided to go to church with them. I experienced my very first real encounter with God when I accepted Him into my life as my Lord and Savior. This was the day my life was changed forever!

The late summer of 1994 is when my ex-husband and I first met. And this was also around the time I'd given my life to Christ and had joined a church not too far from where I lived. As I begun to attend church on a regular basis I began to grow in the things of God. I started to learn about who God was and what He meant to me. I also learned God's voice. He spoke to me through his Word, through many gospel songs that ministered to my spirit, through prayer and fasting, and through preaching during Sunday morning service. Everything about me started changing, my outlook on life, my talk and my walk. I was becoming a new creature in Christ. The old me passed away and all things were made new when I got baptized in Jesus Name!

One thing that hindered my growth and stifled my belief was sin, and it was ever present in my life. I was always reminded of my past and who I was from the people around me. The constant reminders made me not love myself. They made me think I was unlovable by God and by anyone else who tried to love me. My heart and mind were full of the negativity I received growing up. I thought I was worthless and useless. Even though I'd given my life to Christ, I didn't understand I had purpose and that all I endured in my marriage was preparing me for my destiny and the call God had for me.

I latched on to the Bishop and Pastor of the church I went to. They were my parental figures during this time since my mom was in another state, and since I didn't have a good relationship with my dad. They took me under their wings as if I were their child and showered me unconditional Godly love, a love I'd never experienced before. God placed them in my life for me to receive spiritual guidance and wisdom. I served in their ministry for about fifteen years. I learned what it was like to live for Christ and to be sold out to Christ as a young adult. I also learned how to be that wife who stood by her husband's side no matter what happened.

There was the time I was attacked by my ex-husband because I didn't have dinner prepared for him when he got home from work. He always found little things to start an argument over. I was about 8 months pregnant with Faith and was suffering with a terrible case of acid reflux. Everything I ate came right back up, causing me to vomit frequently throughout the day. Not being able to keep food down zapped all my energy. I remember moving around the house in slow motion, almost to the point where I thought I would pass out. And on top of this, I had to look after Destiny. In the midst of him yelling and screaming, he grabbed me, slammed me against the wall. Then he picked me up and body slammed me to the floor. I was frantic, screaming and crying for him to get off me.

As I was scrambling to get from underneath him, he began to choke me. I recall looking into his eyes as I was gasping for air and desperately trying to escape his wrath! I felt myself fading fast! My big belly was my weakness and was preventing me from pushing him off me. I could see the rage in his eyes, and I could hear Destiny's faint cry as my eyes began to slowly close. Destiny saw the entire incident; she was crying as she watched her daddy attempt to choke me the life out of me. At some point he snapped back into his right mind and released the tight grip of his hands around my neck. I laid there trying to catch my breath. I was terrified! For a moment I thought he was going to kill me. Thank God an angel intervened, and my life was sparred. Once I regained my strength, I grabbed Destiny and retreated to our room and locked the door behind me!

It was evident that he'd been drinking from the smell of the alcohol that wreaked through his pores. Drinking made him somebody different, someone I didn't recognize……it made him a monster! Drinking fueled his rage! He would become so infuriated with anger sometimes, that it would be hard for him to come back down to his normal self. He would punch out walls and yell at the top of his lungs. His alcohol addiction caused him to become verbally and physically abusive to me. As the years went on, he got more and more comfortable with violently putting his hands on me and the kids. I learned how to cover him with love just like the bible said in

1 Peter 4:8: And above all things have fervent charity (love) among yourselves; for charity cover a multitude of sins.

Only the people who were close to me knew what was happening in our marriage. It was so much going on that when the truth finally did come out, no one believed me or believed what was really taking place. No one believed he could do the things I was accusing him of. Because of my love for the Lord and my children, I stayed in an abusive marriage. I didn't want to put my children through what I'd gone through as a child. My parents divorced when I was 3. I grew up without a father in the house and it was very hard for me.

I remember praying to God on many occasions, asking Him to fix the issues we were having. I wanted God to pull me out! I wanted Him to deliver me from the hands of mine enemy (Psalms 31:15). I was so desperate that I wanted to take the kids and run but didn't know where to go and who to turn to for help. Everyone who saw what was going on, always expressed their opinions, but no one wanted to get involved. I didn't know how I would take care of three small children alone. I was so used to depending on him to take care us. He was everything to me! Along with my kids, he was my family. I knew I couldn't call my dad because of our unpredictable relationship. I felt as if I would fail at being on my own and that I wouldn't make it without him. I'd finally had enough after many years of being abused and was looking for a way out.

One night I sat and talked to a very dear friend of mine for about an hour while sitting in a grocery store parking lot near my home. She really allowed God to use her for the purposes of ministering to my soul in my desperate time of need. I cried as she told me how strong I was and how I could make it with the help of God. I just needed to find the courage within myself to believe in myself. She also told me my life wasn't over and God had something better in store for me. She encouraged me to hold on because my change was coming and that I should seek God for the answers. I don't know if you have ever been gripped by the spirit of fear before, but if you haven't, it will make you do some crazy things like stay in an abusive marriage and deal with a boy who is trapped in the body of a man.

My children had no stability at all. In the thirteen years that we were married, we moved over ten times. Every time it seemed like we were settled into one house, we were moving to another house or apartment. It hurt my heart to see my kids cry when we had to move. As fast as they would make friends in one school, they would have to start over with making new friends in another school. Their dad squandered money like he squandered his time. I didn't know where the money was going or what he was doing with it. Later, down the timeline of our marriage and after my divorce, is when I found out that he'd borrowed over $5,000.00 from my mom without my knowledge and never paid it back. It was one thing after another with him.

One of the most humiliating times I'd ever experienced with him was when we got put out of our house because he had not paid rent in three months. We were looking to purchase a home and found a great lease-purchase option through our realtor. The house was a three bedroom, two and a half baths with a sunroom and huge fenced in back yard. The girls shared a room and Winston had his own room. This house was perfect for us.

During this time, I was working at the IRS as a Data Transcriber. I would get paid every two weeks and would give him my entire check to assist with the house bills. I was a licensed hair stylist on the side and whatever money I made from that, I kept for myself. My mom would also send me money from time to time just because that's the kind of things she would do for her only daughter.

My mom was so proud and happy for us that she decided to furnish the entire house, except for our bedroom. She bought the kids brand new bedroom sets with matching comforter sets. She also purchased a brand-new living room set and dinette set for the house. The house looked wonderful once she got done decorating! We decided to set the sunroom up as a mini hair studio where I was able to do my clients' hair. Everything was perfect for about 7 months and then all hell broke loose! While my ex-husband was out doing God knows what, I got a phone call from the owner of the house stating that we had to give up possession of the house because the rent hadn't been paid in three months and he hadn't spoken with my ex-husband in a while. I immediately came to his defense because I thought he was paying the rent every month on time. So, I took his word for it when I really should have been asking for receipts and checking bank statements. The owner and I went back and forth for about 30 minutes and the conversation finally ended with me begging him not to put us out. I hung up the phone in a panic and with furious anger!

I called my ex-husband and began to question him not paying the rent. He had every excuse you could think of and finally, after him getting tangled up in his lies, he blurted out the truth. He stated he didn't pay the rent because he got into with the owner during our first month living in the house. He decided to hold on to the rent to teach the owner a lesson. I asked him what in the hell was he thinking and what was he trying to prove? And what lesson was he trying to teach to the owner of our house. He had no words for me. He called the owner and tried to plead his case, but the owner refused to take the $3,000.00. I was devastated! I didn't tell the kids that we would have to move because I knew they would be heartbroken from the bad news. My ex never told me the owner gave us until that Friday to be out of the house.

The up and coming weekend our church had a conference in the city. While we were away at the conference, the owner hired some movers to come and put our belongings outside on the lawn for all who drove by to see. It was raining that day and all our stuff got wet and ruined; our clothes, furniture, the kids' toys, pots and pans, televisions, etc. It just so happened that a neighbor called while we were at the conference to warn us. I sent the kids home with a friend so they wouldn't have to see their things outside on the lawn in the rain. I remember pulling up and seeing everything we owned on the front lawn. My spirit was broken and ripped to pieces. I couldn't believe he would be so egotistical to allow this to happen. He didn't care how I felt nor the kids. He was only thinking about his own selfish intent and motive. That was the moment I made up in my mind it was time to plan the next chapter of my life. And that would be a life without him.

One Sunday morning during church service, the Bishop called all the married couples to the front of the church. He spoke a word from the Lord and told all the couples if the men (representing the heads of their homes) didn't line up and get in tune with God, some marriages were not going to make it. The Bishop also spoke to a few select men in private conversations while standing up there. He told the select men that God was calling them to a forty-day fast and shut in (spend the night at the church). During this forty-day fast God wanted to speak to them concerning their walk with Him and their marriages. My ex-husband was one of the men God was calling to make this sacrifice. This was the day that God began to expose things in my marriage that were not like Him. The more God exposed the worst things got between my ex and me! We argued so much that I no longer wanted the marriage. I knew in my heart of hearts that it was truly was over. I was tired of his shenanigans and wanted to be done with the marriage.

The blatant disrespect grew more and more. He had women calling my house looking for him. They were texting him all times of the night. He got so bold that he even went on a trip to Florida with one of them. Things were crazy! Amid the craziness, I was able to move forward with my plans to leave him. While my husband shut in at the church, I began my preparation and search for a new place for me and the children to live, a place without him. I was also seeking God for guidance and direction. In seeking Him, God began to remove the fear that once gripped my heart, the fear that made me intimidated, and the fear that had me believing I wasn't going to make it.

About a month after we stood in front of the church, two of the elder women prayed with me one night during bible study. God spoke to my heart through the prayer and told me He'd already given me the plan and that He wanted me to trust him no matter the outcome. On the forty first day (after the shut in), my kids and I were preparing to move into our new apartment. I didn't have the credit, nor did I have the money, but God told me to have faith and trust Him. He led me to some apartments in Covington and He gave me favor with one of the ladies at the leasing office. The kids and I moved in the following week after God spoke that word to me. My ex-husband moved in with a friend from the church. This was the official start to our separation.

I needed to talk to someone about the separation and how I was feeling, so I called my dad. We discussed the reasons why I chose to go this route. He was not supportive at all. He told me he didn't agree with it because he saw the damage it caused me over the years when him and my mother separated and divorced. I guess I was in denial when my dad asked me was I sure I wanted to leave their dad since I told him we were separating to work things out. Separation usually meant that things were over. He also stated that in order to work things out, we had to stay together to deal with the issues within our marriage. But I begged to differ with him. I felt that if we separated, I would have the time I needed to figure things out, time to reflect on my marriage and see if it was worth the heartache and pain I'd endured and suffered through and through for thirteen years. I wanted to see if the marriage was salvageable.

When I thought about all the times he cheated on me and abused me, I should have left a long time ago. But I didn't because my love for him ran deep down in my soul and this unhealthy love for him was rooted like the roots of an old oak tree. We were one flesh, mind, body, and soul. The humiliation I suffered behind his cheating angered me. Many people in the church knew about his infidelity and never told me. I didn't find out how reckless he was with his cheating until after our divorce. According to God's word the only grounds for divorce was marital unfaithfulness. Well at least that's the way I understood this scripture: Matthew 19:9, And I say unto you, whosoever shall put away his wife, except it be for fornication, and shall marry another, committeth adultery: and whoso marrieth her which is put away doth commit adultery adultery. I knew this would be my opportunity to throw up the deuces and walk away!

The last three years of our marriage were so unpleasant. I toiled with the decision to leave because of my faith and belief in God. I worried about what people would say. And to think, the shame that came with it made it harder to leave. Here it was two God-fearing people couldn't figure out how to get pass their problems and work through the issues within the marriage. As I stated in my introduction, it takes two to tangle. I just could not fight alone, and the battle was wearing me out emotionally and mentally. When you consider what the bible says about marriage, it is supposed to be a lifetime commitment. Underneath the surface of everything that happened in our marriage, I knew it was over for me.

After the children and I moved into our new place, I wasn't sure if God really opened the door for me to leave. I questioned it for many months after. Being saved came with a lot of mixed emotions at the time of my divorce. One minute I was mad at God because He allowed me to go through some horrible things during my marriage, things that I had never gone through before. And the next minute I was happy that a way of escape was made for me. The main reason I decided to call it quits was because of his unwillingness to change for the betterment of the marriage. His rage was so strong and fearless and with all the death threats, I felt like one day I would meet my demise. I didn't want to leave my children motherless and in the hands of someone else to raise. After all, God gave them to me and wasn't nobody else going to raise my kids like me! I didn't want my girls growing up thinking that the way they saw their dad treat me was love and I didn't want my son growing up thinking that's how you treat women.

There was another time when we were at church and one of the women, he was cheating with came to church to confront him because she found out he was married. Now mind you, I had no clue he was even cheating. But the whole time we were at church, he seemed nervous, he kept stating that he needed to leave because he had some work to do and he needed to take me and the kids' home. I just didn't understand why he was acting that way. The truth didn't come out until about a year after my divorce when a friend sat me down and gave me the "tea" about what really happened that day. She knew the girl he was cheating with and she was the one who stopped the girl from confronting him during service. Although she knew the girl, she had no idea that the girl was messing around with my ex. I was blown away by the information my friend shared with me!

It was another time I caught him in the act of cheating, and I wasn't happy about it either! On this night, my ex-husband told me he was going to hang out with some of the men from church since the women's department was having a Pamper Me party. The planning committee for this party decided to bring in a massage therapist, a hair stylist, and a nail and feet technician to pamper all the moms and grandmothers for their hard work. And I enjoyed every moment of it! Once it was over, I decided to go and get something to eat on my way home. The chicken place that I loved oh so much was closed so I had to go somewhere else. I cut through the parking lot that was located next to the chicken place and lo and behold, my ex-husband's truck was sitting in front the local sports bar we sometimes would go to.

As I drove down the aisle where the truck was parked, I saw shadows inside the truck through the tented windows. It looked as if someone was in the truck, but I couldn't tell, so I pulled the car into the space in front of the truck, got out of the car, and slowly approached the driver's side door. The closer I got to the window of the truck, the more the shadows appeared to be real people. The foggy windows made it hard to see who was inside. I finally realized that it was my ex-husband kissing some other woman. They were so into what they were doing that they didn't even notice I'd pulled up and was standing at the window.

Anger instantly took over me, and I began banging on the windows of the truck, yelling for him to open the door! He jumped up so fast and fearfully looked toward the window right at me. He looked as if he'd seen a ghost! The lady he was with started screaming hysterically as I pulled him out of the truck. He was frantically trying to explain the situation, but I wasn't listening. He was caught red handed and couldn't lie his way out of it like he'd done in the past! I can recall punching him in the face a few times and slapping him before I zoomed off in my car and headed home! He immediately put the lady out of the truck and followed me. When he got home, we argued for the rest of that night. I couldn't believe he had the nerve to try to plead his case. He was not allowed back into our bedroom for months. He tried talking to me, but I didn't want to hear it. I was fed up with all his bulls#$% from over the years and I needed to get away from our volatile, emotionally draining, abusive marriage. The very last time he put his hands on me came when my children and I moved into our new apartment after the separation.

Price of Freedom

Freedom is defined as liberation from slavery or restraint or from the power of another. We are never truly free from anything in life, ourselves, or anyone else until God saves us and fills us with his precious spirit. Freedom comes when we are no longer captive in our minds and thoughts. I was free from my ex-husband because I no longer physically lived with him. But he still had a strong hold on my emotions and my mind. I was mentally trapped with no way to escape. I was bound by my fears and all the negative thoughts running through my mind that he'd spoken over my life. Freedom comes with a price and what price would I be willing to pay to be truly free...

A new chapter my in life had begun. It was such freedom and peace to be in my own place; a place I was proud to call home. It was a small cozy two-bedroom apartment where the kids had to share a room but we love it! It had new carpet, new appliances, and freshly painted walls. It even had a balcony. No more sleepless nights, no more verbal and physical abuse, and no more unstableness. It was time for my children and me to have a normal life. It was time to breathe in a fresh breath of life, for our new beginning was now a reality. We had to learn to adapt to life on our own without their dad; which meant I had to take care of them all by myself. It was very challenging in the beginning, but we adjusted with no problems. I had to retrain their minds when it came to discipline and how things would work with just us four.

I'd just started working a new job three weeks after moving into my new place. I was grateful for the new job but it was not enough money to make ends meet. So I decided to get an evening part time job at the local McDonald's across the street from my apartments. The location was so convenient because it allowed me quicker access to the kids. Lord knows I didn't want to leave them home alone while I worked at night, but I had no other choices. By this time Destiny was in the 5th grade and she'd become responsible enough to have a key to get in the house after she and her siblings got off the school bus. I would leave their after-school snacks on the kitchen counter. The rules were for them to come in, eat their snack, do homework and chores, and then they could watch television. There was no going outside, and neither could company come over while I wasn't at home.

The kids made lots of friends from the apartments within the first month of us living there. I also managed to make a couple of friends that were single parents like myself. Since I was new at single parenting, I leaned on them for advice and moral support. As time went on, we became like a little family. Our kids spent the night at each other's homes from time to time. Sometimes we all even ate dinner together and took the kids on family outings. When I gained trust in my new friends, I told them about my dissolved marriage and estranged ex-husband. They too, came from abused marriages and husbands who cheated on them. From our life experiences, our bond grew stronger. I was in my own place, making my own money, paying my own bills, and taking care of my kids on my own. Things were finally starting to look up and then this happened…

In the last chapter I told you how there was one last time my ex-husband put his hands on me. Well he had to move out of the apartment he was living in because his roommate's lease was up, and the roommate decided to move back to his hometown. He paid his last month's rent and he left. He allowed my ex-husband to stay there for the last couple of months of the lease. Since the separation, my ex started drinking more now than he was drinking when we were together. He would call me sometimes and I could tell he'd been drinking from his slurred speech. He loved talking about how he wanted me and the kids back and how he wanted us to be a family again, but I knew it was the alcohol talking. He often times cursed me out and threatened me if I didn't take him back and let him move in with us. I could always tell when he was drunk. He even decided to go to the Bishop of the church where we attended and talked to him about it. Of course, the Bishop agreed with him about him moving back in with me and the kids. Now mind you, he still had about two weeks left in his friend's apartment.

Once again, during a Sunday Service we got called back up to the front of the church. I was told to let him come back home so that we could work on our marriage. In my mind, I knew it wasn't time because we'd only been separated for a few months and I didn't feel like he was ready to rededicate himself back to our marriage. But out of obedience to my leader I allowed him to move in with me and the kids. Oh boy did this turn out to be a huge mistake! That day after service he went to where he'd been residing, packed his bag, and showed up to my apartment at about 9:30pm very intoxicated. I had this detestable feeling in my stomach about letting him in the door. He staggered in the door smelling like he had drunk a keg full of beer. I became angry, but I didn't say anything because I didn't want to start arguing with him. My dwelling place was peaceful, and I wanted to keep it that way!

Thank God the kids were asleep, and I was glad he didn't wake them. I showed him where my room was and the shower. I refused to let him lay in my bed while he smelled so bad. I laid down and tried to fall asleep while he was in the shower, but I couldn't sleep. My spirit was disturbed and unsettled because I didn't want him at my house. I heard the water shut off in the bathroom He dried off, put on his shorts, and got in the bed. I moved to the edge of the bed, hoping to avoid his touch. He grabbed me and pulled me to his side. I snatched away and got out of the bed. He instantly got mad and started yelling at me. Getting him to leave was nearly impossible! So I told him he had to sleep on the couch. I needed to rest up for work the next morning. I went in my room and locked the door behind me. He antagonized me for the rest of the night with all that banging on the door.

Finally, the morning came, and I got up to get ready for work. It seemed like he'd been up all night waiting on me to awaken because as soon as the light came on in my room he burst into my room. Usually I'm in and out of the kitchen trying to fix my lunch and make sure the kids were up getting ready for school. But this particular morning I was afraid and really didn't want to deal with any crap from him. The plan was to get dressed and get kids up before I left to go to work, but that morning didn't go as expected. I stayed in my room until I finished getting dressed. Once I was done, I made a mad dash out of my room to the kids' door. To my surprise they were already up. Their dad woke them up early so they could eat breakfast before getting on the bus. They were glad to see him, and he was glad to see them! I headed for the door to leave for work and he immediately followed me out of the door to my car. He began to pick a fight as we were walking down the steps because I wouldn't let him in the room the night before. I didn't understand how he became so irate in that instance.

As I was getting in the car, he jumped on top of the hood and started making threats towards me. Fear came over me, the same fear that used to grip my heart when we were together. I could see that same rage in his eyes like all the other times, especially when he would choke me. So, I locked the car doors and started to drive off in order to make him get off the hood. I could see him running back up the steps to the apartment. I began to pray to God for the covering and safety of my babies. After I got done praying, I called my kids to make sure they were ok. Destiny answered the phone and told me they were ok and that he was getting ready to walk them to the bus stop.

I remember him calling me all day, blowing my phone up! My boss was hounding me because I could barely get any work done. I dreaded going home. I knew it was going to be trouble, especially since I was ignoring him and not taking any of his calls or responding to his text messages. I tried to think of somewhere to go to prolong my drive time home, but I had no need to stop anywhere nor did I have anywhere to go. The tears would not stop flowing as I drove home because again, I didn't understand why God was allowing me to go through the same thing I went through before the separation. I thought I'd gotten away from the violence but as you can see, I had to deal with this fool again! All the uncertainty had me petrified and what happened next was not unforeseeable!

I arrived at my apartment complex and waited for the gate to open. All I kept thinking about was how this fool was going to act when I got home. The gate finally opened I slowly drove through. I lived in the back, so it took a couple of minutes to get back there with the all the speed breakers you had to go over. I pulled into my parking space and sat in the car for a moment to gather myself. I didn't know what was going to happen when I got upstairs. I was dealing with a crazy man whom I was very afraid of, especially after the anger he displayed earlier. I took my time getting out of the car and walking up the steps. My heart was beating so fast with anxiety and fear. As I placed the key into the keyhole, he snatched open the door, grabbed me by my shirt, and pulled me into the house! He slammed the door and started pushing me around and attacking me. The kids ran out of the room because they heard us tussling around in my room. I yelled for them to go back in their room and lock the door, but they were too afraid to leave me alone. Somehow, we ended up in a full-blown fight! Usually he would push me around, but this time was different! I felt like I was fighting for my life, my kids, and the many times he ever put his hands in me!

All the other times he jumped on me I never fought back because he always had me pinned down, choking me. But this time I had to send him a message! I have had a few fights in my life with girls growing up, but this is the first time in my life I ever had to fight a man! He was swinging on me with closed fist. My face was taking a beating as he had me backed into the corner of my room. The rage I saw in his eyes this time was a different kind of rage, one I'd never seen before. He had a look in eyes as if he was going to kill me! My eyes quickly panned around the room to see if it was something close by me to pick up. I spotted my cell on the floor and decided in that split second to pick it up. When I came back up my eye caught a jab! So, I took my cell phone and hit him in his face and to my surprise it busted his lip! The hit startled him so much that he stopped punching me. I made a mad dash for the room door. And as I was crossing the threshold of the door, he grabbed my ponytail and yanked me to the floor! He tripped and fell on top of me and wrapped his hands around my neck! My arms were trapped under his knees so I couldn't move. I began to gasp for air and was trying to scream for the kids to call the police!

I saw my son run from across the room, he jumped on his father's back, and started punching him. He was screaming and crying and asking his daddy why was he doing this! His dad grabbed him off his back and threw him across the room! I couldn't believe what I was seeing! Winston hit the wall so hard I thought his back was injured. My ex-husband got up off me and ran out of the front door in a hurry to escape because the police were coming! My son managed to get back up from the rush of adrenaline and ran back over to we're I was laying in the living room to help me.

I could hear the sirens over Destiny and Faith loud cries while they were on the phone talking to one of my good friends. She is the one who called the police to come to my house. I told Destiny to hurry up and lock the front door. As she reached to lock the door, their dad ran back in the house! My heart dropped to the bottom of my stomach! I thought he was coming back to finish me off! I saw my life flash before my eyes! I gained enough strength to make it to the kitchen to grab the biggest knife I could find out of the drawer. Instead of him coming to finish what he'd started, he ran in the room, grabbed his bag and his keys, and darted back out of the door. I was so relieved. I put the knife back in the drawer and leaned on the counter for a minute to catch my breath. I made a mad dash to door and locked it. I grabbed the kids and we all hugged. I didn't care about hiding my tears this time. We'd just experienced the battle of our life.

The police finally made it up the steps and to the door. The bang of their fists knocking on the door scared us. We were all shook up! Faith opened the door for the police. They came in looking around the house. By the way they were looking, they could tell a struggle had ensued. They were staring in awe at me and the kids. One of the cops calmed us down and told the kids to have a seat on the couch. They were still crying, and I wanted to console them, but I knew I had to talk to the police about what had just happened. My hands were trembling due to the fact of me being in shock. I thought me and the kids were going to die! There was one officer writing the police report and another officer taking pictures of my battered and bruised face. They asked me if it was ok to question the kids about the horrible ordeal we'd just been through. I wanted them to talk to the police because usually in the state of Georgia when there is a case of domestic violence both parties involved get locked up. Allowing the kids to tell their side of the story saved me from getting locked up as well. I'm glad their dad left because we both would have probably been going to jail that day.

As I heard the kids began to recall what they witnessed, I started weeping. My heart was so heavy and full. I wanted to be strong for them, but I just couldn't do it. My babies sat maturely and told the police their version of the story. I was proud of them. I tried to smile through the pain, but my smile was lost in my struggle. I glanced at the picture the officer took; the woman in the picture didn't look like me. She had a busted lip and nose dripping with blood, a black and blue eye that was halfway closed, a rosy red swollen cheek and jawbone, and a purple whelp across her nose. I also noticed that her neck was bruised with handprints of the man that choked her. I instantly ran to the bathroom and looked in the mirror! That women in the picture was me!

Overwhelmed with emotion, I gripped the sides of the sink, dropped my head, and began to sob. My scars were not only emotional and psychological, but they were also visible. I looked like a boxer who'd lost the worst fight of his boxing career. I felt broken; grieved in a sense that I'd lost a part of me in our marriage and in this fight. The realization of the control he had over me through the years hit me like a ton of bricks and I fell to my knees. Once again I'd asked myself where God was! I know I read in His word so many times about Him saying He will never leave me nor forsake me! But I felt alone and abandoned! I thought God was supposed to be my protector, but I didn't feel protected! It felt like He opened up the gates of hell and let all those demons out to hurt me and my children! It seemed like God didn't love me because of what He allowed me and my children to suffer through! I was angry at God! This whole experience was so awful and devastating!

The officer saw me curled up and sobbing in a fetal position on the bathroom floor. He slowly picked me up and made sure I was ok. I asked him if the kids were alright and he assured me that they were. He told me to wash my face and come back out to sign the police report. It didn't matter how many times I wiped my face, I couldn't wash away the guilt and shame caused by the bruises or the insecurities and emotional scars that were caused by years of abuse. The kids and the officers were sitting on the couch when I walked out of the bathroom. I signed the police report and the officers left. As he was leaving, he handed me his card and told me not to hesitate to call him if I needed him. The kids and I went to my room to lay down. We didn't talk much. We all fell asleep from exhaustion of fighting off that demon monster.

Bag Lady

Becoming single for me was like getting a new lease on life. Singlehood represented and presented the opportunity for me to find myself, the opportunity for me to re-discover the women that I'd become and bury the little girl that everyone held me to. I wanted to prove to my family, my ex-husband, and my fellow church family and friends that I could handle this task like a champ. I thought I had everything together and under control, until I got on the dating scene and realized I was still carrying heavy baggage from my childhood and from my dissipated marriage.

Newly single and ready to mingle! Not even sure if that's what people were really saying, lol! It felt sort of strange trying to get back into the dating world. I had no clue of what I was doing, being as though I was married throughout my 20s. That's the time when you as a young adult are supposed to be able to find yourself. Nope, not me! I was married at the ripe and tender age of 20. I didn't know anything about life at all! I was "green" and still wet behind the ears, sipping on Similac, as my elders would say! The last thing I needed to be doing was trying to be a wife to someone.

I was carrying a whole lot of baggage from my childhood and teenage years filled with disappointment, low self-esteem, and mental anguish. My divorce meant that I was free from all the pain I endured over the years of being unequally yoked with someone that I barely knew anything about. He hid is inner demons behind the mask of Having It All Together. Being so young and naïve, I didn't recognize the signs of someone who had unresolved issues with his mother while growing up. I didn't recognize the signs of someone who witnessed physical and verbal abuse being done to someone he loved while growing up. I didn't realize I was dealing with someone who was damaged goods. I honestly didn't know what I was getting myself into.

My ex-husband would always tell me that if I left him, nobody would never want me because I had three kids, a ready-made family. He made it seem as if I was doing myself a favor by staying with him. After hearing this for years, the thought of no one wanting me began to take root to my heart and became a part of me. Those very words killed what little self-esteem I had left. I remember the first time he put his hands on me. We were riding on the 285-bypass headed to work in Conyers to Bio-lab, Inc., the place where we met.

As I was driving, I noticed headlights frantically flashing at me. Now in my mind I was trying to figure out why he was flashing his lights, signaling me to get off the expressway! So, I got off on Glenwood Ave and pulled into the Mrs. Winners parking lot and waited for him to pull up. After waiting on what seemed like forever, he finally pulled up. He hoped out of his car in a rage. I'd never seen that look in his eyes before. I was almost afraid to get out of the car.

As soon as I stepped foot out of the car, he ran up to the door and began shaking me profusely, asking me why was I looking at the guy in the car next to me while I was driving on the highway? I didn't have a clue as to what he was referring to and I asked myself, now why would I do that, especially if I knew he was trailing behind me! I stood there with this dumb founded look on my face. I felt myself getting angry, trying to find the words to say without adding fuel to the fire. So, I asked him what he was talking about. How could I have been looking at some guy while I was driving on the expressway going at least 65 mph?

All of a sudden, I felt this burning sensation come across my face. Out of my peripheral view, I saw a man running across the street from the gas station, yelling, "Hey man what are you doing! Why did you hit her?" By this time, I was in a state of confusion and scrambling on the ground to find my glasses. I didn't even realize he'd hit me. He slapped me so hard my glasses flew off my face and landed on the pavement. Still in a state of shock, I got back in my car and drove off. Tears of anger and frustration streamed down my face. I was in total disbelief that he hit me. This should have been a sure sign to break up with him, but my tainted views of love made me stay in the relationship.

During the year of my separation and about a month before my divorce was to be final, I figured I was ready to get back on the dating scene again. Now any normal person would give themselves time before throwing themselves back to the wolves. I thought about going to get some post-divorce counseling, but I quickly dismissed the thought because I wanted to forget about the pain I was feeling. All the violence from my marriage and drama from my childhood may have caused some unforeseen trauma that I'd suppressed over the years. There was something about being by myself that really disturbed me. I always felt like I needed a man in my life. This feeling derived from not having my father as a constant in my life. Girls need their dads because they teach them all about boys and men. Fathers are supposed to steer their daughters in the right direction and offer guidance when needed, especially about men. But I just didn't get this from my dad. Not saying that my mother did not do this because she did.

My mother supported me no matter what I did or didn't do. But it's something about that daddy's love that grips a young girl's heart forever.

As I got older, my connection with my dad faded. We went through our ups and downs, but I never really felt that daddy/daughter connection with my dad. Somewhere on the road of Life, it was severed. That lost connection had me looking for love in all the wrong places and choosing all the wrong men. I always felt a sense of rejection from my dad. While I was going through the beginning process of my divorce, I remember a conversation with my dad where he let me know how disappointed he was with me, my life, and my decision to divorce. I never really talked to my dad about the things that went on in my marriage. The physical and verbal abuse my children and I endured was so real and it made me afraid to tell anyone. It seemed like my dad had the perfect life. So, I kept my dark, dirty laundry to myself.

Growing up we lived by this rule: what happens in this house stays in this house. I also lived by that same rule in my household as well. My dad already had in his mind how a marriage was supposed to be and how I was supposed to be as his daughter. When I grew up and did not become the daughter he envisioned in his mind, I knew I failed him. His actions toward me reflected his disappointment. Regardless to say, my dad and I have a different relationship since my brother passed away. I get more hugs, kisses, and I love you' now than I ever did.

Just thinking about my divorce, my past failed relationships, and my rocky family past, maybe I did need to go and talk to a therapist. Maybe this would have helped me get to the bottom of the unresolved issues I had and suppressed pain in my life. My life issues could not have appeared at a worst time, a time when I started to explore the dating world and find myself as this newly found single woman.

The idea of dating wasn't so exciting anymore because I hadn't dealt with the issues of my past, my failed relationship with my dad and my failed marriage. These issues were deep seated and rooted in my heart. And I too, hid my inner demons with the mask of "Having It All Together" from everyone I knew. I didn't know how to deal with the shame and guilt of being a God-fearing woman and having gone through a nasty divorce. I felt like my church family didn't understand and had let me down, I felt like my dad didn't have my back, and my friends had gone through enough trying to be there for me. My ex-husband took them through hell and back. He blamed them for the breakup of our marriage. He lied to everyone who would listen about how my friends and I would run the streets and was never home to take care of our families. He even lied and said that I was romantically involved with one of them! Oh, the lies he would tell! His mind was so twisted and delusional! He didn't want me to have any friends. He tried his best to pull me away from my family. At one point, my dad actually believed him!

One time I tried to run to my father's house to get away from my ex but he had already beat me to the punch. By the time I got to my dad's house, he'd already called and told Dad all these lies about me and my friends. My dad actually listened to him and questioned me about what he was told. It hurt me so bad as I sat there in an uncommunicative silence listening to my dad recalled my ex's lies. This made me realize that if my own family didn't have my back then who did. I knew at that moment I was on my own and had to figure out how I was going to get through this situation.

No matter how much I tried to block out my past and my resolved marriage, I couldn't. They consumed every fiber of my being, every moment of the day. The thoughts plagued me like a disease that caused an epidemic! So, I found a way to suppress those awful memories. I knew nothing about the dating world. And I quickly learned and adapted to what it was all about. I used the internet as my tool to meet men.

I remember joining different dating sites, searching for men with similar back grounds and common interests as mines. I would post the most recent pictures of myself so that the men on these sites could see what I looked like. There was even a section where I could tell them all about me, with my newly single self! Of course, I embellished the truth just a little bit. Hell, I'm sure they did too! Loneliness and desperation had me seeking attention from anyone who would show interest. I had a huge hole in my heart and needed to fill it with whomever would help me forget about my past. Since I couldn't get validation from my dad, I looked for it from men I found on the dating websites I visited. Now I know to some, this idea of meeting men on the internet was crazy, but it was the norm to those who were casually dating and exploring their options. Honestly it was so dangerous that initially, it made me afraid to join any of the dating sites. But I soon got over that fear.

A week passed before I got my first hit from someone on MySpace. When I opened my inbox to see who hit me up, I had several messages from several different men. It was only one who caught my eye though. I was very skeptical about opening the message. I'd watched too many Lifetime movies, lol! Let's just say that he left his number for me to call him. The initial attraction between male and female is always physical at first. I clicked on his profile picture. He was an average looking kind of guy with no unique facial features. While scrolling down his profile page I saw a few more pictures of Mr. MySpace. I clicked on each picture, one by one to get a closer look. He was dark-skinned with a slender build, standing at about 6'3 in height. I absolutely love a chocolate brother who is tall, dark, and handsome. Mr. MySpace clearly missed the handsome part but just from what I'd read, it appeared that he had his life together.

So, I began to read the "About Me" section on his page. He was 40 years old, with no children, and had recently gone through a divorce. He owned a lucrative construction business in which he started from the ground up. He graduated from Florida A&M and played basketball while in college. In his spare time, he liked to read, watch football, and play golf. He also traveled a lot, searching out new ventures for his business. I have to admit, I was very intrigued by the message he left and wanted to get to know this guy. When I finally got the nerve up to call him, that one phone call led to us talking for about 4 months. I wouldn't even call it "dating." Mr. MySpace and I went on a few dates. Just from our conversation, I could tell that he wasn't being completely honest about what was really going on with him.

My B.S. radar was up because of what I went through with my kid's father. He seemed to be the idea guy but "seeming like" and "actually is", are two different things. I found out some things within those 4 months that I was not pleased with. He had a porn addiction and I honestly didn't want to get myself wrapped up into a man who was dealing with this. His addiction to porn reminded me of how my ex-husband cheated on me time and time again. So, I figured that his addiction would have eventually led to cheating or something worst. And the more and more I thought about it, the more I became turned off. I remember reading a relationship column where this lady's husband dealt with the same problem and they ended up divorced because all the issues the porn addiction caused. The lady talked about the countless nights she spent crying about it. She also mentioned how she would catch him up in the wee hours of the morning on the computer looking at porn. It devastated her. And I just couldn't see myself going through this type of torture with Mr. MySpace.

The relationship with Mr. MySpace was short lived and I was left disappointed. I blocked him from my page and never spoke with him again. Looking at the spiritual side of things, I was moving too fast. The bible says in:

> *Proverbs 3:6 to acknowledge him in all thy ways,*
> *and He shall direct thy paths.*

I was driven by my lustful desires to please my flesh instead of acknowledging God concerning this man. Too many times as a teenager I fell into the same trap of being led by the spirit of lust, and here I was as an adult, repeating the same bad behavioral patterns. I was in a back 'slidin' state and I'd put God on the back burner so that I could appease my flesh and just "do me" for a while.

When I first came out of my divorce, my heart was wide open and vulnerable. I didn't give God the time He needed to take me through the healing process. I left the church right after I divorced. I was always under God's covering, but I was out of His will. I was spiritually blind to all of the traps Satan set for me. I couldn't even hear God speaking. I completely tuned God out because I wanted to do what I wanted to do. Since I got married so young, I missed out on that time I needed to find myself. So, my thirties was dedicated to my finding myself.

Life Lesson

Reflecting on my experience with the Mr. MySpace, I concluded that getting back into the dating world was something I was not ready for. Dating him made me realize I'd been away from the dating scene too long. I was out of touch with the rules of the game. My mind set was still set to "marriage" mode, but I was in the dating world as a single woman. I could not conduct myself as if I was married, while living single. My guard was down, and I was wide open, setting myself up to get hurt time and time again. Before marriage I never really had a chance to date. I moved out of my dad's house at the tender age of 18, ready to see what the world had to offer me. A year and a half later, I was in a relationship, so I thought. Early into the relationship, signs of infidelity showed up. I was too naïve to see what was going on.

Six months later, I was married. Being as young as I was, I missed the essence of finding one's self and how a woman was supposed to be treated by a real man. The physical and verbal abuse started about a month into the marriage. I was too ashamed to tell anyone about what was going on, so I dealt with it. I was taught as a child when things were going on in the home, you keep those things to yourself and you better not tell a soul. I painted the picture of a perfect marriage to my family and friends, but on the inside, I was dying a slow death. As the years passed by, I became accustomed to the violence. I thought it was a normal part of life for couples to fight. I carried all this baggage with me after my divorce. There was no way in hell I should have been trying to date anyone! Fear of being alone drove me to want to pursue Mr. MySpace despite my baggage and inexperience with dating. I never stopped to look at the warning signs in the road. The broken pieces of my heart shattered into smaller pieces. The pain was unbearable. Instead of dealing with the pain, I began to drink, smoke, and party every night of the week. My life was in a downward spiral, headed down a path of destruction.

The Pain Inside

The pain inside I could no longer hide; the guilt I felt because I knew the love wasn't real. The many times I saw you face to face, the pain inside was hard to erase. Your eyes told the story of deceit and lies that you could no longer hide. The communication and love making was not the same. I noticed things between us clearly changed. I couldn't fault anyone, for I was to blame. I could no longer look at our picture in the frame. The pain inside was all so real; how would this broken vessel heal? There were so many concrete walls surrounding my heart; I feared giving love a new start. I built a fortress around my mind; it forced my thought process into a whimsical blind. It was imperative to my existence that I break free! Or this pain inside would snuff the life out of me...

A year passed since my divorce and I found myself still dealing with my unresolved emotions. I didn't allow myself to grieve after I signed on the dotted line. My mindset went straight into "single and ready to mingle" mode. I failed to allow God to deal with me concerning my divorce. And being honest about how I was feeling during that time was essential. I was very angry with God because I didn't understand how my life got turned upside down and ended up in shambles. I questioned God on numerous occasions, wondering why I had to go through this. I knew the spirit of divorce was a generational curse on both sides of my family and I wanted to be the one to break the cycle, the one who defied the odds!

Although I came from a broken, dysfunctional family, I wanted more for my kids and myself. I was determined to stick it out, but all the fiery trials and tribulations came to be too much for me.

Psalms 51:17 says, the sacrifices of God are a broken spirit: a broken and a contrite heart, O God, thou wilt not despise.

Even though I didn't quite understand what that scripture meant at the time, I was truly broken and dealing with a contrite heart. I felt alone and none of my friends and family knew what I was going through. Neither could I turn to my church family because some of them took sides and I trusted no one. I felt so alone.

I would hear stories from different members in my church that saw my ex-husband out with other women, and no one told me anything. They all would say that it wasn't their business but that didn't stop them from gossiping about me and my situation. I could hear the whispers in the spirit, I could feel the glaring stares from the different ones in the church who'd taken his side. They were quick to judge the situation and my actions but none of them walked a mile in my shoes. None of these same people never took time to ask me what happened, they just took in what he told them and ran with it! Even when I walked into the church the day after he jumped on me with shades on attempting to hide my swollen, bruised and battered face, some of them still didn't believe the monster he was! The feelings of betrayal by some of the people in my church overwhelmed me. It seemed like some of them got a kick out of seeing my marriage fall apart!

I was left looking like a fool, standing by this man's side and didn't have a clue about nothing that was going on with him. It felt like God didn't care that I was heartbroken over losing my marriage to the world, meaning, divorce is something that is so easy for the world, but for someone who is saved and a follower of Christ, divorce shouldn't have even been an option. But for me, it was the only option! I prayed, but did I really believe God could heal the wounds or mend the broken fences? So much had happened that caused me to take my eyes off God and focus more on what I was going through. I began to turn a deaf ear to God. I didn't want to hear what He was saying to me. My spirit was so cold, preventing me from feeling the presence of God in my life during this time. I was slowly dying a spiritual death that no one in the church saw. The void and emptiness killed me spiritually.

After dealing with all the turmoil from my divorce and the division it caused between our mutual friends in ministry, I left the church. My kids and I left the people we grew up with, the people we were connected to in the spirit. We left my spiritual parents who nurtured me and took me in as their own. We left friends that were more of a family to me than my own family. I say "we" because I too, started going to this church when I was about eighteen or nineteen years old. My kids were born into this ministry, so they were leaving behind their friends that they knew from birth. I wanted to get as far away as possible from my ex-husband and the church.

I couldn't stand the sight of looking at him and seeing him smile, especially with knowing that he was hiding the real him from our church family and everyone who knew us. I wanted him to hurt like I hurt! I wanted him to suffer like I was suffering! The brokenness hurt like hell! And there were many, many days where I would sit and cry, blaming God for how I was feeling. I became very depressed and sad. Thank God the kids were visiting their dad for the summer. I didn't want them to see me hurting and always sad and crying all the time. I stayed hidden in my apartment like a recluse, a hermit in its shell. The only places I went was to work, the liquor store, and home. I would meet up with the weed man from time to time to buy weed. Smoking made me forget about the pain inside...

It took me several months to get out of this slump I was in. Church became obsolete in the lives of me and my children and because I'd given up on God, I didn't want no parts of the church I once knew or any other church for that matter! I needed time to deal with my internal conflicts and grieve my marriage without feeling the convictions of hearing God speak through His Word being preached, or concerning the state I was in. I wanted to take pleasure in sinning, and I wanted to be in denial about the way I was feeling! Holding on to the baggage and feelings of bitterness became a sense of security for me. I owned the way I was feeling, and no one could take that away from me. My mind and heart were closed off to God. I'd posted a "no trespass" sign to the Holy Spirit on the door of my heart. The devil had me thinking I could make it without God. My heart was surrounded by a big huge gigantic wall, like a castle that was surround by its towering walls. The only way anyone was getting in again was if I let them in, including God.

The struggles of being single made me grow up and mature. I learned how to manage my household, budget money, and bring stability to my kids' life. Stability that they were missing from all the times we had to move when I was with their dad. Not having a man around made me adjust to doing simple things that most men handled in a marriage like taking out the trash, mowing the yard, and washing the car. At an early age, my son learned how to do these things and he did them with joy. Doing these things and watching my son perform these different tasks made me realize what I wanted out of life and what I wanted in a man. I was no longer the little girl that everyone knew me to be, the push over, the timid, shy little girl. I went from living with my parents and having no voice to living on my own, raising three kids alone, to having a voice, and being able to freely express myself. I demanded a certain respect from men now that I was single. When you have been through so much bad, you gain a sense of entitlement that things are supposed to go a certain way. I knew how to manipulate men to get what I wanted from them. The hurt and pain I was holding inside caused me to treat men wrong. I treated them how they treated me and all the other females like myself. I used them the way they used me. I didn't care if I hurt them or not! My ex-husband ruined it for any man I dated after him.

I finally got the hang of being single and parenting three kids alone since my divorce. Now that we were all settled into this new lifestyle, I decided to go back to school to study computers. I always wanted to pursue a career in IT world ever since my dad bought my first computer when I was in the 7th grade. It was love at first sight, me and that Commodore 64! From that day forth I had an enlightened and heightened interest in computers and what made them work. I'd worked at the IRS for about 8 years now and my time there started to wind up. I knew I didn't want to be stuck there forever, so I started researching schools which had degree programs in computers. For once in my life I wanted to do something for myself and pursue my childhood dream of becoming an IT Professional!

I lived in the shadows of my ex-husband and his dream of owning his own construction business. All my dreams where placed on the back burner to becoming a wife and mother. Nothing mattered more to me when I got married than family. And that's what I focused on, even after my divorce. Having the weight of caring for three children alone on my shoulders was very challenging and I didn't want to let my kids down or make any mistakes that would cost us our newly found freedom. Working a full-time job and going to school required me to be away from home a lot. On top of these two demanding obligations, I still had to find time to manage the kids' extracurricular activities as well. And not even to mention, my personal life, and my dating life!

My time at the IRS ended and I'd decided to attend school at ITT Technical Institute. By this time, we were living in McDonough, Georgia. We'd just moved in our first house and was settling in quite well. Life as an adult college student and raising a family presented its challenges but it wasn't anything that I couldn't handle or manage. I pushed myself for the two years it took to obtain my Associates degree. The flip side to this was, I sacrificed time that I know I needed to spend with my kids to complete my degree. School nights were Mondays, Wednesdays, and Fridays from 6pm to 10pm. This schedule changed every semester.

On Sundays I would prepare dinner for a few days, so the kids would be able to eat on the nights I wasn't home. Destiny stepped up to the plate once again to look after her sister and brother while I attended school. I know it probably was too much for a twelve-year-old to handle but she exuded a lot of confidence and ability to get the job done. Even though she called me quite often to tell me what was going on, I still knew she could handle the burden that was placed on her. Destiny became a latch key kid around the age of seven or eight. She learned responsibility at an early age. For some reason I knew I could always count on her. Maybe in her little mind she didn't want to let me down. I always thought she was strong in character and I pulled strength from her. There were so many times she would tell me, "Mommy it's going to be ok." I guess that was the Lord allowing her to encourage me during those rough times.

She'd seen and heard too much of our bad situation when her dad and I were married. We argued a lot when she was small. Like most kids who would watch their parents arguing, she would cry. I remember times when she would go find her sister and brother and hug them to console them because they would cry too. I would watch in amazement as she wiped their tears away. Faith and Winston leaned on her for her strength and support as well. It was funny to hear her try to discipline them. She sounded a lot like me. The times I thought she wasn't listening she really was listening. I must admit, she held things down during the times I had to work and go to school.

Mr. NFL Himself

Having spiritual discernment can save us from a lot of unnecessary trials. Looking through the eyes of lust led me down some dangerous roads. My own selfish and fleshly desires fueled the lustful spirit that was operating in me. It made me enter a relationship a lot like my marriage, except without the physical abuse. But the verbal abuse and lack of respect was ever present. I was dealing with yet, another man, like my ex-husband who had "mom" issues. I was so blinded by lust that I ignored the warning signs from the Holy Spirit...

I'd just started dating this guy that we will call Mr. NFL. And yes, he played professional football for a while after he graduated from a very prestigious historical black college. I met him while working for the federal government. He was about 6'4 in height, dark-skinned, handsome, and had major swag out of this world. He was from a small town off the coast of Georgia. His southern charm captured me. I would see him in the hallways at work from time to time but never really paid attention to him until he introduced himself one day. By the end of the conversation, we'd exchanged numbers. That same feeling, I had after meeting Randy, was the same feeling I had after meeting him. His cologne lingered in the hall as he walked away. It gave me chills and butterflies in my stomach! Like every new budding soon-to-be relationship, we talked almost every day. And of course, we saw each other at work most days. His work area wasn't too far from mine, which made it easy for me to walk over to his cubical to see and talk to him.

Through conversations with different friends who worked with me, I found out that we both were invited to the same cookout the following weekend. I was looking forward to going because I now had a definite reason to be there. Usually, my home girls and I would ride together but this time we drove separately. I didn't know what the night would bring, and I wanted to be free to leave when I got ready to leave. I don't remember what I wore that night but whatever it was he couldn't stop staring at me and me at him. He was looking so fly, matching and color coordinated from head to toe. We mingled and danced a little bit at the cookout. As the cookout neared the end, he suggested that we go and hang out for a while longer without the crowd. He wanted to spend some alone time with me, and it was my pleasure to oblige him. He chose the spot and I led the way.

He followed me to Barnacles, a sports bar and grill in Lithonia I frequented regularly. I had a home girl who bartended there, so I knew I could drink and eat for little to nothing. We talked on the phone as he trailed me, so he wouldn't get lost. He said he wasn't familiar with this side of town. As we pulled up to the spot, he told me to wait in the car until he got out, and of course I was trying to figure out why. I waited anxiously until he got out. He ran over to the door to open it as he saw me reach for the door handle. I couldn't help but smile because of his kind gesture. He knew that would win brownie points with me.

I got out of the car and we headed towards the entrance. I could feel him looking at my butt as I walked in front of him. He opened the door to the restaurant, and we walked in. We found two empty seats at the bar right in front of my friend's station and sat down. I introduced him to my friend whom I referred to as my little sister. And this night started our off and on, two-and-a-half-year relationship.

To my surprise the night at the bar ended up with him coming to my house. I know you are probably thinking we had sex, but we didn't' sleep together. My friend loaded us up with so many drinks that we both got drunk! He was so drunk he couldn't even drive. I was also drunk but not to the point where I couldn't drive. After a couple hours of dancing, drinking, and eating, I took his keys and walked him to my car.

I had to lay the seat all the way back because of how tall he was. He was so wasted, that he fell asleep as soon as we got in the car. The funny thing about this was, I usually didn't do things like this. He was still a stranger to me. But I don't know how I would have felt if he'd driven himself home and something would've happened to him. It was obvious that he trusted me because he slept while I drove, with no clue of where we were going. I had to make the long drive back to Covington by myself. I blasted the music and let the windows done to keep myself awake. The only reason I brought him back to my house was because the kids were with their dad for the weekend and I didn't have any idea of where he stayed and never got a chance to ask him. The alcohol had him inebriated!

I made it a rule not to intertwine my dating life and home life together. I was very protective of my children and I didn't want them to get attached to him, especially not knowing how long he would be in the picture. We pulled up to my apartments about twenty-five minutes later. He woke up asking where he was as I led him up the stairs to my apartment door, staggering the whole way. When we got inside, I gave him a glass of water and an

Ibuprofen and suggested that he sit down on the couch. I told him to get comfortable because that's where he would be sleeping for the rest of the night. With a crazy look on his face, he busted out laughing, as if he had other things on his mind. He asked for a blanket and went to sleep.

I locked my room door behind me and took a nice cool shower. I was in disbelief that I allowed this man to come to my house without really knowing him like that. Another one of my rules was to not let the men I dated know where I lived. Being single also made me more scared and more cautious than usual because of all the horror stories I'd heard and watched on Lifetime TV! My hormones were raging from all the drinking and from me grinding on him while we were on the dance floor near the bar. I wanted to have sex with him so bad, but I was afraid of what he might think of me afterwards and plus it was too soon. Having self-control during a moment like this was crucial. Didn't want to give him too much of myself at this stage of getting to know him. The cool shower did me some justice! I got out of shower, threw on some boy shorts and a tank top, and got in the bed. I drifted off to sleep thinking about the man that was laying on my couch in the living room.

Morning came, as I could see and feel the sun peeking through the blinds. I knew He was up before me because I heard movement coming from the living room, but I decided to lay there a few minutes longer. After a while, I got up to brush my teeth and wash my face before going out to speak with him. He greeted me with a hug and a kiss on the forehead. That was his way of thanking me for not letting him drive himself home. I told him it was no problem and would do it for him again if I had to. He offered to take me to breakfast to show his appreciation. I could tell by the way he smiled he was much obliged! He had the prettiest white teeth and smile I'd seen on a man besides my dad!

I ran in my room to get dressed while he freshened up in the guest bathroom. Afterwards, we headed out to go to breakfast. We ended up eating at the IHOP near the bar we went to the night before. I got a chance to find out a little more about him. The conversation was refreshing and pleasant. Neither one of us expected the night to end up the way it did. He admitted halfway through breakfast he wanted to sleep with me, but he also wanted to respect my wishes of not crossing the line with him. He said this was the first time he'd ever went home with a lady after leaving the bar and did not have sex with the same night. I couldn't believe what I was hearing! I didn't know if he was running game or really trying to make me feel special. He was so charming and had a way with his words. I grew a fondness for his personality in that moment. He paid for breakfast and we headed back to his car to drop him off. He was very talkative during the ride. He explained to me how he really enjoyed our night out. I had a great time as well and it showed outwardly. I was smiling and blushing hard! I really liked him, and I wanted him to know it! It'd been a while since I dated anyone, so I welcomed his charm, corniness, and wit with open arms!

Riding home after the wonderful breakfast we had gave me time to meditate on the things that Mr. NFL openly expressed. He had a bachelor's degree in Business Finance. He also played college football on a full ride scholarship! He too, came out of a bad marriage. Both of us made sure not to go into any details regarding why we divorced. Opening myself up too soon would have me made me vulnerable and that was one radar that I was trying to stay off. Vulnerability for me meant I was weak, and I didn't want to show any signs of weakness! I wanted things to progress with him, so that part of my life remained off limits until I was ready to share. I was so looking forward to this new prospect.

In the beginning of the relationship Mr. NFL and I talked almost every day. As time went on, I learned the real reason he was single. His ex-wife divorced him because of an act of infidelity that resulted in a pregnancy. I remember riding in his car with him while he ran some errands. And as we were riding, we came to this neighborhood I was not familiar with. I quickly learned that this was where he used to live with his ex-wife and by the looks of the yard and house, she obviously still lived there. It was a nice cozy cul-de-sac with about five houses. He stopped in front of the house and suddenly took off, making a screeching noise with the tires. He drove in circles around the cul-de-sac several times. Fear was racing through my heart! The look in his eyes reminded me of my ex-husband and how he looked when he became enraged. After about 2 minutes of frantic circling, he snapped out of his trance and drove out of the neighborhood.

This is when I realized he had some real issues with anger, and I became afraid and very leery in that instance about continuing to pursue a relationship with him. He started ranting on and on about how he still had clothes at the house and other belongings she wouldn't give him because of the restraining order she filed against him for stalking her. HOLD UP! WAIT A MINUTE! PAUSE! Restraining order? He never told me about a restraining order, I thought to myself. I can believe it to be true after what he just did in that cul-de-sac! This was one of the clearest warning signs of all the warning signs from God, considering what I just gone through dealing with my ex-husband. But I ignored the big red flashing lights that were going off in my mind and in my spirit because I was still interested in him.

I remained quiet out of fear, not knowing what to say, for my mind was blown! All kind of thoughts were running through my head like, was he really a stalker? What made him snap like that? Would he be the same way with me? The uncertainty alone stirred up feelings of anxiety within me. I asked him if he wanted to go have drinks to calm his nerve. He agreed, and we went to Taco Mac on Highway 138 in Stockbridge. We parked near the back of the place since the front parking lot was full. Before we got out the car, he leaned over, gently grabbed my face and turned it towards him. We softly kissed for what seemed like an eternity! He reached for my hand as we walked towards the restaurant.

His gesture was a gesture of reassurance, him letting me know he would be there for me and him saying he needed me to be there for him. And because of this very act of reassurance, I felt a sense of obligation to him. I wish I could explain it so you could really understand what I was talking about and feeling. I immediately let my guard down and embraced this moment of him letting me into his world. I'm pretty sure you can imagine what happened after we left the restaurant. These first few months were like a heavenly bliss. He wined and dined me every chance he got and spoiled me with lavishing gifts and money. It all seemed too good to be true. The Bishop of the church I left once told me when a man gives you his money that means you are special to him and that there was nothing in the world, he wouldn't do for you. I knew I was special to Mr. NFL, but our relationship was never clearly defined. As you read you will come to understand what I mean when I say things were not clearly defined.

Relationship Blues

We were about six months into the relationship and things were going smoothly until one day out of the blue his son's mother contacted me via a phone call, talking about he would never commit to me because he was still messing around with her and a host of other women. I was so confused while trying to figure out who she was and what was going on. She had major attitude out of this world! I was curious as to how she got my number. She told me she went through Mr. NFL's phone while he was asleep and noticed a few calls to and from my number. She said she figured I must be somebody worth calling since the call log revealed the number of minutes me and Mr. NFL talked each day. I couldn't believe the nerve of this heffa! I guess she figured since she was 'baby momma', she could do as she pleased. I did my best to remain calm as we talked. She proceeded to tell me who she was and a few details about the relationship between her and the man I'd been kicking it with for the last six months.

She disclosed that they had a six-year-old son together which I already knew about. And how she was over his house a couple of weekends ago. She told me they slept together while she was there. She also stated that she met him in college where they dated. She began to tell me how he was never faithful to her while they were in school. I was still angry from her calling me, but I made sure to cover it up while talking to her. The one thing I learned when I was married to my ex-husband was to never "to take it there" with the other women because nine times out of ten, they had no clue about me and their Mister's home life. And I refused to argue with her over the phone because for one, I was at work and two, I didn't know if she was telling the truth. At the point she took a breath, I jumped in and let her know that if she continued to raise her voice, then I was hanging up. She piped down and wanted to hear what I had to say as well.

We talked for what I know had to be about 45 minutes. Once we got off the phone, I called Mr. NFL to discuss this phone call I'd received from his baby momma. He explained to me that she was over to his apartment, but not for the entire weekend and that she was there picking up some clothes he'd bought for their son. I didn't know who to believe! Because of that vulnerable state I was in that I tried to avoid in the beginning, I still ended up getting hurt. I felt in my spirit that she was telling the truth about everything and confronting the man who was supposed to be my guy, didn't make me feel any better either. I knew he was not being totally honest with me. Now you might say I should have left him alone, but I didn't. I allowed myself to fall in love with him, he had me, my heart, mind, body, and soul. It was nothing I wouldn't do for him and him for me. We had this unexplainable connection and bond that most people would have never understood.

A year into the relationship, he asked me to get a passport because he wanted to take me to "exotic places" and these were his exact words. I rushed out to get a passport in hopes that this trip to "exotic places" would happen soon, only to find out it was all lies and that he never planned on taking me anywhere! It was just a line he used to keep me interested in him. He ended up taking someone else! Again, this should have been a warning sign to walk away but my feelings, time, and resources were too invested. He'd just moved in with me and the kids to help out financially. And to add icing on the cake, the kids had gotten attached and grew to love him. I could not walk away! There were just too many factors involved. I found out that the girl he went out of town with was someone who also worked at the same government agency we worked for. Since I didn't know who she was, I took to Facebook to play detective and do some investigating. By the end of my investigation, I realized I'd seen the girl before in the hallways were we worked but didn't know her name at the time nor did I know who she was.

After about 2 weeks of looking into the situation, I decided to inbox this mystery woman via Facebook to talk about Mr. NFL. We talked over email for the entire day. She asked me did I want to talk about it over the phone, so we exchanged numbers and I called her. We handled the situation like two grown women. She told me they'd been friends for the last year and that she knew he liked her, but she wasn't too sure about dating him. She did admit that since he lavished her with expensive gifts and free trips, she would stick around and enjoy the moment while it lasted. In my mind I'm thinking, who goes on a trip with someone they really don't like in that way. But what I didn't tell her is that there was a missing condom from a box of twelve that he used while they were on their trip together. But she swore to me that she didn't sleep with him. I was so confused. I found out later that she did sleep with him. I guess she didn't want to tell me because in her mind she figured it wasn't my business. Even after this little situation, I still didn't put him out or break up with him. I absolutely loved this man and was tired of his ish' but not tired enough to end it with him.

This is a prime example of an ungodly soul tie. The phrase "soul tie" is not exactly stated in the bible, but the bible does speak on ungodly relationships. Proverbs 1:10-15 reads: My son, if sinners entice thee, consent thou not. If they say, Come with us, let us lay wait for blood, let us lurk privily for the innocent without cause: Let us swallow them up alive as the grave; and whole, as those that go down into the pit: We shall find all precious substance, we shall fill our houses with spoil: Cast in thy lot among us; let us all have one purse: My son, walk not thou in the way with them; refrain thy foot from their path. There is no need for any explanation of this scripture because the bible clearly states children of God should not allow themselves to be entangled with sinners in this manner.

I continued in error and yet again, ignored another warning sign. Things with our relationship started going downhill fast. Meanwhile, I still hadn't met any of his family or friends after almost 2 years of being with him and I caught hell trying to get him to meet my family. All my friends were introduced to him early on into our so-called relationship and none of them liked him. Another warning sign I ignored! He didn't meet my family until the very end of our "whatever you want to call it", since it was never clearly defined as a relationship!

The straw that broke the camel's back was when he came home one night to take a shower then left right back out to go spend the night out with another woman! All while he was staying with me and using my car. And had the nerve to lie about it when I asked him where he was going so late at night! I guess he just didn't care anymore about my feelings or the fact he could get put out of my house over his bad decisions lately. I don't know at what point he lost respect for me and what we had together, our so-called relationship. My investigative skills divulged pictures of him and other women he'd taken with his cell phone. Looking through his phone was a frequent habit because I'd lost trust in him after the baby momma conversation. Let me remind you that the baby momma situation happened six months into us getting together. This situation however, was different for me. I was fed the hell up and could not take any more mistreatment!

I packed all his clothes and belongings and sat them outside on my back porch under a tarp. I called him and told him he had 2 weeks to come and pick up his things. He never showed up, so I brought everything back into the house and sold it all. I made about $700.00 in sales, which added up to the same amount he owed me from the agreement we had with him staying at my house. I'm not the revengeful type but he turned me into the Queen B that most men hate to see coming their way when trouble arises. I'm usually the door matt who allowed men to walk all over me and dust their feet off when they got what they wanted from me. Then they walked out of my life just as fast as they entered it. Not this time! I had to hit him where it hurts! When I walked away, I walked away knowing I didn't lose anything, but a boy trapped in a man's body who still to this day is single and running the same games on other women that he ran on me!

Life Lesson

This is what happens when you ignore the warning signs from the Lord. God didn't give us that "women's intuition" for nothing! I failed to yield to the voice of the Holy Ghost when it would speak to me regarding the many different situations, I went through hell with Mr. NFL. I ended up wasting two and a half years of my life and time with someone who didn't deserve me. I was "putting the cart before the horse" as my elders would say. He didn't respect me and never had any intentions on me being a part of his future. I was a friend with benefits playing "wifey." He walked out of my life with my dignity and my heart. It wasn't his fault that he treated me like this. But what was my fault, was the fact that I for allowed him to treat me as an option and not a priority.

In my desperation for wanting to be loved and wanting to fill that void that God left empty for Him, I simply accepted his foolishness because I didn't want to lose him or be alone. I didn't realize how damaging this was to my children. This so-called relationship was just another let down and disappointment for them as well. They wanted a father figure in their lives that he just wasn't willing to be. We all lost in the end. And once again, my heart shattered into tiny fragments that only God would be able to put back together.

The Birdman

Lust of the flesh, lust of the eyes, and the pride of life will lead you down a path of temptation that will cause you to lose a hold on God. These three sins also open the door to so many other fleshy manifestations, things you never thought or imagined you would do. Never thought I would go so low as to beg a man to stay with me who clearly didn't deserve me nor want me. This ever-present sin in my life and character flaw stopped me from trusting God and waiting on Him to send me the man He wanted me to have...

Casual Dating...I never really understood this term. This is how Wikipedia defines it: Casual dating is a physical and emotional relationship between two people who may have casual sex or a near-sexual relationship without necessarily demanding or expecting the extra commitments of a more formal romantic relationship. Motives for casual relationships vary from person to person. Now this is what the Word of God says when it comes to finding a mate:

> *Proverbs 18:22: Whoso findeth a wife findeth a good thing, and obtaineth favour of the LORD.*

So once again, I was in error because I was looking and searching for "the one." I wasn't even sure if this is what I was supposed to be doing as a Christian woman who was single. Or if it was even right in God's eyes.

I was lonely and desperate, looking for love in all the wrong places, trying to feel a void that only God could feel. How else was

I supposed to figure out what I liked or didn't like in a man? How was I supposed to test the waters? But I did manage to go on a date or two with most of the guys I met. A few of them never made it past the first phone call. There were many dating websites I signed up for during this period in my life. I even signed up on a Christian dating website. Funny thing is, I couldn't tell genuine from phony on either site! Most of the men on these dating sites were liars! Their profiles said one thing but when you spoke with them on the phone, the truth came out. And for me, the worst part of meeting different guys online was that some of them did not look like their profile pictures.

Online dating was like going on a blind date, I never knew what I was going to get when we finally did meet in person. We all know how some blind dates turn out! LOL! I had the opportunity to date many guys but NONE of them filled the emptiness I was feeling. Some experiences were good, and some were bad, but both sharpened my discernment and gave me wisdom going forward. And I learned so much about myself from my many dating experiences. It was during this time I realized I gained self-respect and didn't have to degrade myself or do anything I didn't want to do just to keep a man. I began to see what guys were about and what they really wanted only after a few conversations. Most men didn't want a commitment. They wanted to be friends with benefits or just simply friends. They stood by the fact that they didn't want things to become complicated due to feelings getting involved. I learned how to play the game of dating. It took several years into my singlehood to figure things out, but I eventually got it! I set the standard and tone as to how I wanted my singlehood to flow and how I wanted to be treated. And even though I was doing my own thing, God still covered me.

It is one more guy I want to share with you who negatively impacted my life. We will call him the Bird Man. I thought I had my single lifestyle under control, but as you read the story of the Bird Man you will see the same repeated pattern of bad choices and behavior when it came to men. I met the Birdman at this company I used to work for back in 2012. I'd been out of work for almost a year prior to this job. It wasn't paying much but I welcomed any new opportunity that resulted in money flow! God always reminded me of His Word when it came to the many different situations in my life, despite the fact that I was very deep in sin: Matthew 25:21: His lord said unto him, well done, thou good and faithful servant: thou hast been faithful over a few things, I will make thee ruler over many things: enter thou into the joy of thy lord. Unemployment was about to run out and my God came through right on time with this job!

Within a year of me being at this job is when the Birdman entered the picture. Never really thought about approaching him until I overheard a conversation, he was having with someone about some furniture he wanted to sell. I needed furniture for my family room in the new house I'd just moved to. So, I decided to email him and asked him to send me pictures of the furniture. Instead, he set up a time and day for me to meet him at his storage to see the furniture. We met the following weekend after he invited me to view it. I made sure I had my money in hand just in case I liked the furniture and wanted to purchase it. They day came for us to meet. I don't know why I was checking myself out in the mirror to make sure I was put together, looking good and smelling good! Even though we saw one another at work most days, outside of work, first impressions are always lasting impressions.

His storage was on the other side town and I had to drive almost an hour just to meet him. I arrived there on time just to find out that he was running late. He phoned ahead to let me know he would be pulling up in 15 minutes. So, I sat and waited patiently for him to arrive. Once he arrived, he flagged me down to follow him through the gate to his storage unit. We both parked and got out of the car. For the life of me, I couldn't figure out why I'd never noticed him before now. He stepped out of the car and I was like "d@#$, he fine!", as I thought to myself. Now mind you, I saw him many times at work, but never noticed him. And plus, we didn't work in the same department. I only saw him in passing.

As I approached him, I could smell the celestial cologne he was wearing. And this was the one of the things that instantly attracted me to him! I said hello and complimented him on his awesome smelling choice of eau de cologne. He tried to hide the fact that he'd been blushing, but it was too late! We proceeded to talk more about the furniture. By the end of the conversation, I decided I wanted the sectional couch. I gave him the money and scheduled a time to come back and pick up the gently used furniture from the storage. He wrote me a receipt and told me not to be a stranger. I laughed it off like a giddy little girl, got in my car, and drove off.

That did it for me! Hook, line, and sinker! I took the "don't be a stranger" bait and was ready to be reeled in! I knew this was his way of opening the door for more casual conversation outside of work. I'd already locked his number in my phone from the email he sent earlier that week. I didn't call him right away, but we did text a few times for the rest of the weekend. I was excited about going to work because I knew I would see him there. I picked out the cutest business casual outfit (nothing revealing of course) that

I could find in my closet to ensure a reaction from him. Monday morning couldn't come quick enough! I got up, got dressed for work and hurried to the office.

As I was putting my purse in my desk drawer, I heard him speak. He always walked past my cubical to go to the break room to get coffee. I turned around and waved with this big grin on my face. He returned the sexiest smile I'd seen in a while. He held the door open to the breakroom as if he was inviting me in to come and drink coffee with him. Reading between the lines, I took him up on his offer and headed to the breakroom. We talked for a little bit and went back to our separate desks to start work. I couldn't even focus on work with him on my mind. I found myself heading over to his desk to see him quite often through-out the day. And from here is where it all started. We grew very fond of one another through conversation over the next several months. He wasn't the tallest I've ever dated but his charm and personality made up for his height. Not to mention, he was chocolate (dark-skinned) with a bald head with a sense of fashion, just the way I liked them! And I also liked the fact that he was in touch with his emotional side. And what I mean by this is, he wasn't afraid to cry in front of me. For a man, this is a big thing because most boys are taught at a young age that crying makes them look weak.

Reflecting back on a time that we were riding together one night, headed out on a late-night date. He received a very unpleasant phone call from his older sister. He was the youngest of his two sibling sisters. He hadn't really shared too much with me regarding his family before this call, so I didn't know that they were having family problems. While talking to his sister, they started arguing. The louder he got the more passionate and emotional he became about the conversation he was having. And if I remember correctly, his sister ended up hanging up on him. He began weeping. I didn't know if I should console him or just leave him alone, but soon realized that I didn't have to do anything because he started talking to me first. The last grown man I saw cry was my ex-husband, so to see him in this vulnerable state was shocking.

I sat and listened and waited patiently for an opportunity to speak. As I began to encourage him, I learned he was a believer of Christ like me. I just knew in my heart we would go a long way. I felt at that moment that we made a spiritual connection. It turned me on to see him cry. Not in a sexual way though. It speaks volumes when a man allows himself to be open and vulnerable in front of you. For him to let me see him cry, meant that he trusted me with his heart. He was being emotional and allowing me to witness it took our newly established relationship to another level. Another level that meant I was his woman and he was my man.

Things became official and I wanted everyone in the office to know. One of the biggest mistakes I made during our relationship was letting all of Facebook and Instagram know that we were an item. I posted pictures of everything we did. Letting the world in on what we had, opened the door to a lot unnecessary and unwanted negativity from others who despised our relationship. It also drew the attention of people who had their eye on my Bird Man at our place of employment. I mean, after all, he was a hot commodity and a lot of women wanted him, but I was the one he chose. And we looked damn good together too! His swag was swag-a-licious! It was slim pickins' at the workplace! And I got the finest thang in the building! I know you are not supposed to date people you work with, but I broke my own rules!

Besides us dating, I still had the obligation of witnessing to him. He started visiting my church. He met all my friends and church family. No one really liked him, but I guess I couldn't see what they saw spiritually. My friends and former pastor were always looking out for me. Especially because they knew I'd been through a lot and did not need any extra baggage weighing me down. The Birdman knew he had a call on his life and would always talk about it to me. His deliverance was supposed to come through me because of my connection with God. God wanted to use me to help bring salvation to him and to bring him into the fullness of who God was calling him to be. But I allowed my flesh to get in the way of what God was trying to do with the both of us.

I didn't realize that every time I slept with him; I was binding his soul because of my disobedience to God. Here I was thinking that if we both were going to church; God would look past the fact that we were sinning. I know you might ask why I was thinking this, and you might even say I was crazy for thinking this. The truth of the matter is, I'd fallen in love with him and allowed my feelings to override the Holy Ghost and doing what was right. Since we were looking for engagement rings, I felt that it was OK for us to continue to live in sin even though problems started to arise. In my mind we would be married soon, and I loved him, so it didn't matter that we were having sex before marriage.

We soon started pre-marital counseling with my pastors. The first day of the first counseling session was the last day. Soon after, the issues started. The Birdman started questioning our relationship and questioning if I was really the one for him. His oldest sister was the little birdie that was in his ear and I knew she'd planted that seed of doubt in his head. She would always remind him of my ready-made family and of the fact I couldn't have any more kids. And if this wasn't enough, he began to tell me that he felt he was missing out on life by settling down with me.

I remember a conversation we had where he was reminiscing about his life before I came into the picture. He shared how he would spend the night with one woman one night and then the next night he would end up at different woman's house. I heard all about how he enjoyed clubbing and hanging out in the streets with his friends as his hobby. It became apparent we were on two different pages in life. I didn't club anymore and hanging out with my friends was far and in between. We all had our own personal and separate lives. I also found out about 6 months into the relationship that Mr. Bird Man was creeping with a new girl who'd just started working at our place of employment.

She made it known she was interested in my man and she wanted him, and how she wasn't going to stop pursuing him until she got what she wanted. And it didn't take long for her to get her hooks into him either! There were rumors spreading that she was on a quest to get her prize. It didn't matter to her that we were in a relationship. She threw the bait put out there and he bit the hook! Everyone around the office knew what was going on except me! But oh, when I found out, I went off on him! It was devastating for me because once again, I was left holding my empty heart full of hurt and disappointment. The worst part of it all was that I was left looking like a fool.

I was reminded of my failed marriage and infidelity issues with my ex-husband. You would have thought I would've walked away and ended the relationship, but I didn't. My love for him and my desperation to be with a man superseded his wrongdoing. My feelings on the back burner instead of dealing with them. I knew I needed to move on but part of me felt I couldn't do any better than him. Taking him back meant that I was allowing him to disrespect me all over again. It meant that he basically could walk all over me because I didn't have enough self-respect to stand my ground when he did me wrong. Not dealing with my internal conflicts always showed up in all my relationships, good or bad.

The relationship continued to go downhill like an avalanche, and I knew the end was near. A short time after taking him back, we both got invited to a mutual friend's birthday dinner. While at this birthday dinner, he and the one of waitresses assigned to the dinner party openly flirted right in front of me. I could not believe the audacity of this n**** and the level of disrespect he's shown towards me! As mad as I was, I played it off, trying not to draw attention to myself or the situation. By the time the dinner party was over, we were arguing! And from the looks of things he didn't care that I was hurt. He tried to flip the script on me as if it were my fault. I wasn't the one flirting, he was! His nonchalant attitude was appalling! As we drove back to my place, he let me know that we were over, and that he wanted out of the relationship. I begged him to stay so that we could work things out, but his mind was already made up to leave. My worst nightmare had come true. He walked out of my life just as fast as he came into it and I was left to once again pick up the pieces of my heart.

Life Lesson

Sin and disobedience to God will cause us as Christians to forfeit the blessings He has for us. Here I was once again, a repeat offender of things I said I would not deal with or do just to keep a man. I lowered my standards for the sake of desperation. That feeling of yearning and longing for a man, made me lose sight of myself and the things of God. Even though I took him to church to meet my pastors, so they could discern his spirit, I didn't seek God regarding this relationship. The Bird Man needed to be delivered from the baggage of his past. He too wore the mask of "Having It All Together" and wanted people to think he was doing OK in life. Maybe he would have been the man for me if I would have waited on God through His process of deliverance for the Bird Man. Instead, I allowed the lust of the flesh, lust of the eyes, and the pride of life cause me to forfeit what could have been my blessing, had I waited on God. In my selfish quest to find love, I delayed my own process of deliverance. I was trying to make a relationship work that God had nothing to do with from the beginning. God put him in my path for me to witness to him and bring him to Christ. God didn't put him in my path for me to have a relationship with. Yet again, I failed the test. In failing this test time and time again, I realized some changes had to be made. And the changes that needed to be made had to start with me first.

A Change of Heart

There comes a time in life when you must give up the one thing you love and hold dear to your heart, to obtain what God has for you. For me, God was requiring something from me and wanted me to sacrifice my "So-called Single Life" for a rededicated life with Him and in Him, full of promise and purpose. This sacrifice would build my trust and faith in Him, instead of the men that I put my faith and trust into. I had to be willing to let go of my way of doing things and grab hold to God for the journey ahead of me...

Seatbelt pulled tight, wheels up! I was ready for takeoff! My good friend invited me to come to the jazz festival in Miami for the weekend. It was a much needed get-away where I could let my hair down and be free for a few days. No kids, no bills, and no worries! I'd never been to Miami and I was looking forward to my mini vacation. The plane ride from Atlanta to Miami was very short with no time to sleep. I knew as soon as we hit the city, the party would begin. This was the first time in years I'd gone on a vacation without my children. I viewed it as a time to get away from the pressures of life that were going on in my world. Being single and raising three kids on my own was very difficult. Going from working two jobs to no job, had taken its toll on me. Bills were falling behind, and not to mention, my breakup with the Bird Man was still fresh.

Going to Miami couldn't have come at a better time! It was a temporary escape that put a temporary band aid on my lifelong wound. I was still at a low point in my life after my breakup with the Bird Man. I knew I couldn't return to my bad behavior of using men liked they used me. I had to find a way to cope and deal with my heart ache. The Bird Man hurt me deeply to the point of me hating him for a while. I thought he was the one, the one who would choose me as his wife to live happily ever after. I thought he was the answer to all my "single woman" problems but it turned out that he too, was a big disappointment. He had unresolved issues from his past to deal with as well. Instead of me being the weaker vessel in the relationship, I found myself being a strong tower for him. In the words of K. Michelle and her song: You Can't Raise a Man!

I needed someone to be strong for me for a change. After all the years of being single and carrying my heavy load, I began to weaken and break down, mind, body, and soul. Even though I was breaking down spiritually and mentally, my face was set like a flint like the scripture in Isaiah 50:7 - For the Lord GOD will help me; therefore, shall I not be confounded: therefore, have I set my face like a flint, and I know that I shall not be ashamed. I didn't want anyone to see any weakness in me. I put on the façade as if I had it all together. The truth of the matter is, I needed help and was looking for Randy, my ex-husband, the Mr. MySpace, Mr. NFL, and the Bird Man to rescue me from my sorrows. I was too prideful to turn to my pastors for help, and after the dissolution of my marriage, I didn't trust anyone.

Now, back to Miami! We arrived in Miami early that morning and decided to stop and get breakfast at a local home style eatery before our hotel check-in. I was so excited to be in the city! I'd never been there and all I wanted to do was go to South Beach to see if it was really like the celebrities said it was! And of course, I was ready to go to the jazz festival in Miami Gardens. Heck that was the main reason I was there! We ate breakfast and checked into our hotel afterwards. Even though my body was exhausted from traveling, I wanted to see what Miami had to offer this single mom who'd been mistreated by the men she loved from the time she was old enough to start dating up until her last relationship. I had to be careful not to slip back into my old ways. I honestly was trying to retrain my mind to do things differently. And plus, God started to deal with me regarding the path I was on right before I was invited to go on this trip to Miami.

The first night of the music festival was in a few hours so we had to quickly settle into our hotel and get dressed. I laid my suitcase on my bed and picked out an outfit and some sandals to wear. Considering the beautiful weather in Miami, I chose my strapless red and white sun dress and my red sandals. It went perfect with my fresh haircut that showcased my natural hair! I put on a little make up to complete my outfit and waited for my friend to get dressed. After she finished getting dressed, we called our ride and waited for them pick us up. While waiting, we decided to roll one up and take some pictures. That ganja had us high as a kite flying in the wind, lol! Our ride finally pulled up and we headed to Miami Gardens for the jazz festival.

But before we arrived at the festival, we made two stops. One stop was to pick up the alcohol infused drink concoction from one of my home girl's friend house. And the other stop was to the Dollar Store to find something to put the special drink mix in. We didn't want to spend any money on drinks because we knew they would be pricy at the venue. We pulled up to the venue and found somewhere to park, filled up our containers, and headed to our seats. I was feeling real good right about now. The ganja and drink combination had me floating on the clouds by the time the festival started. I grabbed some food from one of the food trucks and danced the night away until the last music act left the stage.

I know God was not pleased with my current situation but like people say, if you gone sin, do it the right way and enjoy it while you in it! And that's exactly what I did! I guess I was trying to forget about the pain the Bird Man caused me with all the drinking and smoking I was doing. I was so wasted I don't even remember the ride back to the hotel. I woke up the next morning with the same sun dress on as the day before. The hang over was oh so real! I had a major headache which equated to a 7.8 earthquake on the Richter scale and my stomach was churning like you churn butter. I took off the dress and found some shorts and a tank top to throw on and headed downstairs to the lobby for the continental breakfast the hotel was offering.

I had to get some food in my stomach because I was feeling queasy and nauseous. With every step I took my head was spinning and pounding at the same time. But I knew if I didn't get any food in my system, I would paint a pretty picture on the floor with the contents of my stomach! I settled for a couple pieces of toast, eggs, and bacon. I also grabbed a cup of coffee to wake me up. I started to feel much better as I ate my food and drank my coffee. Breakfast was so needed and what seemed to be the cure for the awful headache and hang over symptoms I was experiencing. I made my way back up to the room after about an hour and got back in the bed for a couple of hours.

I woke up to the sounds of music playing in the background. My friend was up taking a shower. I laid there for a minute to gather myself before I got out of bed. Those two extra hours of sleep did me and my body some justice. I felt refreshed and my hangover was finally gone! I pulled day 2's outfit (my form fitting sundress and black sandals) from my suitcase and laid it across the bed. Today's agenda was to do some shopping before going out to the venue for the last day of the jazz festival. I waited for my friend to get out of the shower so that I could hop in. I didn't want time to get away from me. She was already dressed by the time I got out the shower. Our ride was already there. I had to rush to get dress, so we could head out.

We ended up going to a little outlet mall about 30 minutes away to do some last-minute shopping. While we were riding in the car, I received a text from my Pastor asking me to call her when I got a free moment. In my mind, I'm wondering what this call could be about. I was very anxious to find out. I did not want to interrupt the fun I was having with all that nervous energy, so I waited until after the festival to call her. I can really laugh at myself right now because thinking back to that night, I was terribly afraid to call her back! My former Pastor is a prophetess and I thought she'd received this deep revelation from God concerning my life and about me being in Miami. I didn't want her to put a damper on my mini vacation! I was in no position to talk about how I needed to elevate my mind spiritually. Especially being that the first music act was about to hit the stage, and I didn't want to miss it, Fantasia or Neo! Charlie Wilson closed out the night and the festival was over. That three and a half hours was the most fun I had in Miami!

My friend's flight was set to leave directly after the concert and my flight was set to leave the next morning. They dropped my off at a new hotel closer to the airport and headed to the airport to catch their flight back to Atlanta.

God's Request

Being saved means your life is being viewed through a magnifying glass by others. People lay and wait for you to make a mistake, so they can say "You are supposed to be saved!" They can't wait to judge you and to call you a hypocrite. The one thing most people ALWAYS forget is, that you are human and that you make mistakes. Jesus tells us in:

> *Job 14:1, "man that is born of a woman is of few days and full of trouble."*

This means we are born into sin and we are going to make mistakes and fall short of God's glory every day until we are presented faultless before our King in our glorified and heavenly bodies. God wanted me to live a godly, holy life before others. But I didn't realize this until that night I called my pastor back after avoiding talking to her about what I was going through. I found out during that conversation what God wanted me to do. And what she said God had for me to do, changed the very course of my life and put me on a new path going in the right direction...

I decided to give the pastor a call to see what she wanted. She greeted me the pleasant tone she always talked in when she wanted something from you. She proceeded to asked me how I was doing. I told her I was doing fine and that I was in Miami for a much-needed mini vacation. As the conversation went on, she began to tell me how she was glad me and the kids were back at the church and how she has watch me grow spiritually over the last year. She said she was praying for me and what God wanted me to do during this time in my life. Pastor didn't bother me much during the first year of us being back because she wanted to give us time to get back in tune with God and acclimated to how things worked at the church. I also needed to deal with my unresolved feelings regarding "the church" from over the years. The undealt with church hurt caused me to rebel. Sitting in church being judged and criticized made me run away from God.

Going through a divorce while being a born-again believer was very difficult and rough. People we (my ex-husband and I) both grew up with in the church took sides. And when I say people, I mean people who were called to leadership in ministry; ministers, deacons, deaconess, preachers, teacher, prophets. My divorce brought about an unspoken division of some sort amongst some of the members in my church. I really saw who was in my corner and who wasn't. And I also saw who was in my ex's corner and who wasn't. Some people judged a situation they knew nothing about. Some people knew what was going on with my ex-husband and told me nothing. Everyone had an opinion and it's almost as if they all sat back and watched my marriage fall apart.

The church was a place where I thought I was supposed to get help. But instead I got whispers and pointed fingers. The only option I felt I had was to leave the place where I met God, the place where I thought my sin-sick soul was supposed to be healed, the place where Jesus told me to come as I am. But in all my exposed nakedness, my deep open wounds and scars bled with shame and regret. I trusted no one, not even my spiritual leaders. The kids and I left the church for three years and returned under unforeseen circumstances.

Now getting back to the conversation I was having with the Pastor. She also stated it was time for me to get active in the ministry. She told me I was going to be over the Singles ministry. I was flabbergasted by the news and it left me speechless! I asked her was she sure God told her to choose me to take on such an enormous task. She reassured me God chose me for this position. After our conversation, feelings of unworthiness came over me. I had problems of my own! How was I going to lead others? I was so deep in sin that I was drowning! I felt like I had nothing to offer other singles in my church. Yeah, I'd been through some things, but I just didn't understand why God wanted me to be over the Singles' ministry. I couldn't see what God saw in me. And because it was a mandate from God, I couldn't refuse.

That night in my hotel room was spent weeping. I wrestled with this new assignment for about 2 weeks. At the point I decided to accept the commission from God, He begin to deal with me immensely through prayer. I remember praying one night and God spoke to me: "Daughter, give me one year and I will give you the desires of your heart." He spoke to me in the same still small voice He used when I was a child. It was that plain and simple. I woke up the next day with a renewed faith in God because He heard my prayers. I went through my cell phone and deleted every male contact I used to date, mess around with, and hung out with. I also deleted text and voicemail messages. I even deleted the pictures associated with these men, past and present, that I felt would be a distraction and a hindrance to me during this year of consecration. I made a commitment to bring my flesh under the subjection of the Holy Ghost. No more overriding what was right! Play time was over and I wasn't playing any more games with God or anyone else.

I sat my kids down when I got back from Miami and talked to them about the place, I was in. I explained to them what God wanted me to do and how important it was for me to stay committed to the call of being over the Singles' ministry. I also apologized to them for all the mess I subjected them to with being disobedient to the will of God. I know opinions may very when I say this, but I should have never introduced them to any of the men I dated. I gave them a false hope of having a father figure in their lives. They too, were longing to be loved unconditionally and needed the presence of a male authority to help rear them. They didn't fully understand how wrong it was, but I knew better. They were very welcoming to the change.

This type of request from God took dedication and focus. I had to block out all distractions because I needed to be able to hear God's voice clearly. Not saying I was all deep in the spirit or anything, but this was a time of instruction from the Lord. Shortly after coming to a place of acceptance, God begin to deal with me regarding things of my past, mainly, the rocky relationship with my dad and my failed marriage. He also dealt with me about why I would always choose the wrong guys. All three of these issues were tied into one another, so I knew it would be interesting to learn God's perspective on things.

My "daddy" issues ran deep, meaning and the wound in my heart was deeply rooted. Growing up, I never understood what the real issue was between my father and me. He expressed the disappointment he felt when I divorced my abusive ex-husband. It hurt me to the core to hear my dad tell me he was disappointed with my life because he felt as if I hadn't accomplished anything in life. And I felt like he couldn't relate to being in an abusive marriage, divorcing, and raising three kids alone. Reflecting on the many conversations we had, God began to speak to my heart where my dad was concerned.

I knew my dad really loved me, but he didn't know how to show me. He wanted to be there for me, but he didn't know how to make it right. All the attempts with trying to talk to my dad failed. Every time we would plan to sit down and talk, it never happened. Not being able to express myself to him and not being able to get to the bottom of the way I was feeling, caused resentment and anger to build up in my heart towards him. Even though I was not pleased with the way things were going with our relationship, it didn't hinder the love I had for him. When you are a daddy's girl at heart, no matter what is not right, you still consider your dad a superhero!

The only way we would be able to move forward was for me to forgive him. Forgiving him meant I had to let go of everything in my heart I was holding on to. And believe me, there were some very deep-rooted issues and scars! I decided to keep a journal because it was way easier for me to be myself and write my true feelings, knowing, my dad or no one else would see the journal entries but God. I wrote letters to my dad as if I were going to send them to him, but I never did send them. There was one letter that really freed me from the guilt and shame of my past. It allowed me to let go of some things I held over my father's head and I was able to forgive him for not being there during these tumultuous times in my life.

Dear Dad,

I know I haven't been the best daughter I can be. I have made a lot of mistakes and bad decisions on this lonely, rocky road called "life". I never meant to hurt you or disappoint you. I have been holding on to things for years that you've said to me that really hurt me. I was angry when you didn't come to my high graduation due to a misunderstanding we had. I have held on to the pain of you not being there for me when I needed you most. Dad I went through some rough times when I was back and forth between you and my mom, especially as a young child and teenager.

I never told you or anyone about the time I was molested at age five and raped at age seventeen by someone I barely knew. I wanted to call you and tell you so bad, but I thought you would blame me and judge me. I thought you would not look at me the same. I thought you would think I was nasty and dirty. I was so ashamed this happened that I blocked it out of my mind like it never happened. I blamed you for not being there to protect me as a little girl. Being molested did something to me.

It took my innocence and stole my childhood. It showed me a false pretense of love. This situation was traumatizing and ruined my life for years to come. It made me not trust anyone. You and my stepmother judged my behavior for years, but not once did either of you ask me did something happen to me. Everything that went wrong when I lived with you was always my fault. I resented you for not being that listening ear and that sounding board that I needed you to be. As your daughter, I needed to know that I was still and would always be your little princess no matter how old I got and no matter the wrong I'd done in your eyes. I was angry at the fact that every time I called you just to say hello and talk to you, you never would get on the phone to talk to me. You always let your wife do the talking. I found myself questioning my mom about why you didn't want me as your daughter. I blamed you for all the bad I'd gone through with the different boys and men I'd encountered through-out my life. There were things you were supposed to tell me that would have helped steer my decision making when it came to men. Had you just got on the phone and talked to me about men, some of the bad relationships I entered could have been avoided. I needed to feel a father's love from you so that I wouldn't have looked for love in all the wrong places. I'm allowing God to clean my heart and Dad I want to say I apologize for holding these things over your head. I forgive you and I ask you to forgive me.

Love, Sherry

Writing was always therapy for me and this method of expression helped me to dump my past hurts and pains into my journal. There were days I cried a river writing to my dad and other people that hurt me. Feelings I'd been carrying for years were released and I began to experience a freedom I'd never experienced before. I also used this same method to deal with all the broken relationships I had, and the men involved in those relationships, including my failed marriage. Through this process is where God healed my heart and I also reconnected with Him on a new spiritual level. Things in my life began to line up with God's will and what He had for me. My prayer life became stronger than ever, I learned about spiritual gifts I didn't know I had, my knowledge in God's Word increased, my spiritual discernment was sharpened, and my spiritual hearing even tuned in to the spirit of God like never before. I was finally in tune with God. And all of this happened within a year's timing and while I was over the Singles Ministry.

I was able to be an effective leader during this time to a group of singles who came from different backgrounds because I allowed God to lead me and guide me. The weights that so easily beset me once before had fallen off and I was soaring in the spirit like an eagle that soared in the sky! It was a great feeling! For once in my life I could honestly profess I was happy in Jesus and it wasn't because of any man or material thing. It was the true essence of God's unadulterated love and joy that filled the empty void in my heart. I allowed God to endow me with His presence. For the first time ever, I was clearly seeing God's plan and direction for my life. I knew I had a story to tell that would one day help other women who was going through what I'd gone through. My life being viewed under a magnifying glass didn't seem so bad after all. I was no longer hiding behind the guilt and shame of my defeated past. This is when my life truly changed for the better.

Life Lesson

Life sometimes requires us to make sacrifices we really don't want to make in order for us to get what we want. So in the natural, so in the spirit. But when we make this type of sacrifice in the spirit, there is a greater reward because it comes from God. I gave up my worldly single life that brought nothing to my life but heart ache and pain, for a Godly single life that profited my soul in the most fulfilling way. And that hunger and thirst for the things of God filled me up with His goodness. This one decision to rededicate my life back to God was the best decision I could have ever made. It gave me a new lease on life, and I was able to forgive the people of my past and present. I didn't rush this process because I knew I wanted to be totally delivered and set free from all the things of my past that had me bound by chains and shackles. I openly and willingly allowed God to perform a spiritual surgery on my heart which brought about a healing only God can do. The cares of my past often smothered me and sucked the life out of me. For once in my life I was able to just breathe, inhale……exhale. Little did I know that God was setting me up for something great and He was preparing me for my next chapter of my life. Know this, God's plans will always be greater and more beautiful than all your disappointments.

Perfect Timing

We all have heard the saying, "Good things come to those who wait" or "patience is a virtue." I know its cliché but it's true. Being impatient causes unwanted stress and anxiety. I was in a time in my life where I wanted nothing but to please God and wait on the things God had in store for me.

> *Jeremiah 29:11-13 For I know the thoughts that I think toward you, saith the LORD, thoughts of peace, and not of evil, to give you an expected end. Then shall ye call upon me, and ye shall go and pray unto me, and I will hearken unto you. And ye shall seek me, and find me, when ye shall search for me with all your heart.*

This scripture helped me to wait patiently on God and let me know that God had everything concerning my life under control. It also taught me that all I had to do was reach up, God was there all along...

The weekend of weddings was finally here, and the kids and I were prepped and ready to go! It was a time of celebration and coming together of families. A good friend of mine was marrying the love of her life and my brother was marrying the love of his life. As I was preparing for what God had for me, my brother and good friend were also amid planning for their weddings. Weddings symbolize unity and strength in two people who decided to come together to become one under God and before their witnesses. I was glad to be a part of these two awesome unions! I'd just gone through a six-month long process of losing weight, so that I would be able to fit into both of my bride's maid dresses. Not only did I want to feel good, but I also wanted to look good.

I didn't take part in the planning for my brother's wedding. Thank God! Helping plan my friend's wedding was very stressful! However, it was well worth the stress! We started around the same time of my rededication to Christ. I'd just moved into my new house after being laid off from my job. I did not allow my circumstances to interfere with me being there for my friend and her special moment. She texted me and invited me to the first planning meeting which would be held at a mutual friend's house. The entire wedding party was there, and I got a chance to meet them all!

I dropped my son off at football practice earlier that night and headed over to the meeting. I had not been a part of a wedding in years. I was super excited and honored to be one of the bride's maid in two different weddings. I arrived at my destination and rang the doorbell. The door opened after a few moments of waiting, I walked in and followed the host to the family room where everyone else was sitting. Most people I knew, and I'd seen before but there was one face that I'd never met. We would take turns introducing ourselves. I was kind of anxious to find out who this unfamiliar face was. I secretly took notice to this new face as his turn neared for him to introduce himself. I had been inconspicuous, as I didn't want to draw any attention to myself nor did I want anyone to know I was checking him out.

He said his name was Rashad and he was the best friend of the groom. After the introductions, we all headed to the kitchen to grab a bite to eat. While we were eating, I notice Rashad staring at me out of my peripheral view, but I didn't look his way. I had to keep my cool! I was so out of source with talking to guys and dating that I didn't know what to do or say, lol! It was funny to me because he made me nervous. Now mind you, I had not talked to a guy in over a year! I was a tad bit rusty. I headed back into the family room to take my seat across the room, being careful in choosing a seat that was opposite of him. I listened to my friend discuss the process of wedding planning and what the next steps would be. Just hearing everything made my excitement kick into overdrive! The meeting ended after about 45 minutes and everyone parted ways.

While I was saying my "good-byes", Rashad and the groom-to-be walked outside to talk. So, I decided to walk out right after them to do a little ear hustling. As I was getting closer to my car, I heard Rashad ask who I was. This meant he'd been checking me out as well. I got in the car with a smile on my face and drove off. I began to think about the possibilities of dating this guy while I was driving to pick my son up from football practice. Lord knows I didn't have time to be getting caught up with any man and his foolishness! The last thing I needed was another bad relationship!

I was in a good place with my life. For once, I was very happy in the woman I'd matured to spiritually and naturally. My happiness didn't come from a man or material thing, it simply came from my love for God and the things of God. Even the detrimental end to the relationship I had with the Bird Man did not knock me off my spiritual high. Yes, I experienced the heartbreak of a bad relationship, but I didn't let it ruin my world. God was able to quickly restore my peace and heal my heart because I let the relationship go and moved on with life. Most importantly, I forgave him. Plus, how would God bless me with

Mr. Right holding on to Mr. Wrong and all the heavy baggage that came with him? God knew I was ready to settle down and be married again but it had to be to the person God had for me. God constantly reminded me of this scripture:

> *Proverbs 18:22 Whoso findeth a wife findeth a good thing, and obtaineth favor of the Lord.*

I wanted my Boaz to find me. I had no time to waste with the wrong guy.

A few months passed, and we had not had any meetings for the planning of the wedding. I often wondered how Rashad was doing. Since I had not talked to my friend in a while, I didn't have any updates on him. I decided to text her to see how things were going. It took her forever to text back, but she finally did after about 15 minutes. She'd hired a wedding planner to get the ball rolling a little quicker with her plans. She stated things were going well and that she wanted to do a fun outing with the wedding party for the upcoming weekend. I was excited and down for the cause because I would get to see Rashad again, the groom's friend in whom I was so intrigued about. I couldn't put my finger on it, but it was something different about him that sparked my interest. My friend and her fiancé spoke good things about Rashad. And both encouraged me to talk to him.

My friend decided to have a bowling night for the wedding party sooner than later, so we could mingle and enjoy each other's company. The only rule was no wedding talk! Go figure, right? That was perfect for me because my friend was really stressed and passing the stress to the bridal party as well. We all needed a night out on the town! I was so looking forward to this bowling night. Since this was an adult only event, the kids had to stay home. It had been quite a while since I'd gone out to hang with friends besides hanging with the singles from my church. I had about a day and a half to find the perfect outfit. I wanted to make sure I was looking fabulous for the outing. Although this would not be the first impression, but I wanted it to be a lasting impression. I wasn't sure if Rashad was the guy God had for me but if he was, I wanted to look good from head to toe.

The weekend finally arrived, and it was time for the bowling party. My kids were gone for the weekend which meant I was free to have a good time without any worries. I arrived at the bowling alley ahead of the scheduled time. I was the first one there and had to wait on everyone else to get there. My confidence was up, and I'd finally gotten the nerve to talk to Rashad. To my surprise, he showed up to the outing with a date. I felt a little disappointed inside, but I didn't show it. I greeted Rashad and his date with a smile and a friendly hug. I usually don't approach guys first and decided to immediately withdraw my plan to approach Rashad. I retreated to my seat and waited on the rest of my friends to arrive.

I secretly watched his interaction with his date in amazement. He was so attentive and caring to her needs and presented himself to be such a gentleman. This is what I was longing for, someone who would be attentive and care for me whole heartedly. He pulled out her chair for her and asked her if she needed anything. What he did next was also key in letting me know where things stood with her. He introduced her without any title to everyone else who arrived after I did. And to me this meant that they were not together. But I wanted to make sure, so I spent a little time during that evening finding out. My probing paid off! Just as I thought from the way that he introduced her, my inclination was right on target.

The night progressed, and we were into our third and final game. I'd done a great job by not overstepping my boundaries. I respected the fact that he'd brought a date and I didn't want to come off as being desperate or disrespectful to his date. By the end of the night I'd found out what I needed to know. He was single and the chick that came with him was not his girlfriend. The excitement was back, and I regained hope! All is fair in love and war! The wedding was around the corner and I knew I would have another opportunity to talk to him, so I patiently waited.

Meanwhile, I was busy with the Singles Ministry. We'd just started a series study on the Virtuous women in the book of Proverbs. Being a Christian single woman, it was important that I stayed focused on the things of God because I didn't want to lose sight of my worth and all I'd gained during my one-on-one time with God. I'd learned so much about myself during my time of separation from the distractions in my life and during my time of consecration to the Lord. I found strength from within myself that God put in me to stand when times were hard for me. My faith in my Heavenly Father grew stronger because I didn't have to turn to anyone but Him. My prayer life increased and His voice became crystal clear to me. My hunger and thirst for God's word and righteousness superseded my own desires. I understood that He wanted the best for me, and I shouldn't settle. I learned to acknowledge Him in all my ways as He directed my paths.

The rehearsal dinner and wedding were finally here, and I was looking forward to celebrating with my friend during her happy occasion. The opportunity presented itself again for me to talk to Rashad and I was ready. He looked even better that day than he did from the first day I'd met him. He was cleanly shaven and smelling great! He hugged me when he saw me and greeted my children. We all got on the elevator and headed up to the area where the wedding would be held. We both were absorbed in conversation with one another instead of paying attention to the wedding coordinator during the rehearsal. He seemed to be a very interesting guy I wanted to get to know a little more about him, which meant we would have to keep in touch with one another after the wedding.

Since we'd finally gotten a chance to talk, I thought this would be the perfect time to invite him and the other single groomsmen to some of our singles' functions. They were very accepting of the invitation to come and hang out with us. Rashad took this opportunity to ask me for my number and of course I gave it to him without hesitation! After we exchanged numbers, Rashad walked me and the kids to my car and watched me drive off into the night.

The Courtship

> *Proverbs 31:10-12 Who can find a virtuous woman; for her price is far above rubies? The heart of her husband doth safely trust in her, so that he shall have no need of spoil. She will do him good and not evil all the days of her life.*

Did my Boaz find me? This is what I was sure hoping for. But in the back of my mind I still was thinking that I was unworthy because of all that I'd gone through. Even in all our unworthiness, God will still allow the person that is meant to be in your life view you as worthy...

It felt like I was living life in a dream or fairytale. Rashad and I hit it off so well at the wedding that I decided to invite him as my date to my brother's wedding. Rashad showed me such an awesome time at the first wedding that I knew he wouldn't mind escorting me to my brother's wedding. I usually wouldn't bring guys I was dating around my children or family because I didn't want to offer any promises or false hopes to anyone. And I never knew if they would stick around or not. But I had a different feeling about Rashad and didn't want the feeling to end! We both took off from work the day after my brother's wedding that happened to be on a Sunday. We were tired from the long weekend. Who wouldn't have been tired from being in two weddings in the same weekend? Family was still in town and I wanted everyone to meet Rashad. My parents invited us to come to breakfast at their house on Monday morning. I wanted my family's honest opinion on what they thought about him. They got a chance to interact with Rashad at the wedding, but I wanted them to see him in a more personal setting.

I woke up that morning and called Rashad to see what time he was coming to my house so that we could leave. He told me he'd just left his house and would be to me in about 20 minutes. It seemed like it took him forever to get to my house! Or, maybe I was just a little excited at the thought of seeing him again! Once he pulled into my driveway, he parked his truck and hopped into my car. We rode for an hour before we arrived at my parents' house. During the car ride he started talking about his life and his background. We talked about how he connected with my kids at the wedding and how we all danced the night away! He told me he had two kids, a daughter who was 11 and a son who was 14. He was a Route Salesmen at a local trucking company and had been on his job for about eight years. He attended a local mega ministry for the three years and counting, which was a plus for me. I always wanted a man who loved God and attended church regularly. I asked him how his relationship with his mom was. This was important to me because you can always tell a lot about a man who has a good relationship with his mom. If he treats his mom well than I know he knows how to treat a woman. And remember, most of the men I dated had "mom" issues, so I had to make sure Rashad was clear of this.

We arrived at my parents' house around 10am. My dad was in the beginning stages of cooking breakfast and had no problem asking Rashad to jump in where he fit in with the cooking. He leaped at the chance to make a good impression with me! And trust, I was attentively and eagerly watching! He blended in so well with my family! They all loved him which was no surprise. He had a great personality and seemed to be a people person. The men finished cooking breakfast and we all sat down to eat. Rashad and I were a good fit, hand in glove. I know, you say it was so soon, but when you have chemistry with a person, then that's just what it is, chemistry, and with chemistry, time doesn't matter. Just seeing him interact with my family so well was a sense of satisfaction and it put a smile on my face. I was fathoming the thought of a future with Rashad, but I knew I had to pump my breaks! I didn't want to fall too fast. There was something different about him and I took my time getting to know him.

After coming off a year and a half man free hiatus and spiritual cleansing, I could recognize game from any man. God removed the blinders that were created by the illusion of real love from Satan. God had given me spiritual insight when it came to men and whoever God was sending my way, had to come correct! I knew how to discern a lie from the truth because I was able to hear God's voice clearly and audibly. I felt as if God had given me this hidden single lady superpower or something! I also had my "woman intuition." But ain't nothing like having a direct line to God when I needed Him the most!

I could tell by the way Rashad handled me that he had a good relationship with his mom. Rashad had to be on his "A" game when dealing with me. I did not need anyone who would bring me down or back to that place of insecurity and depression I suffered with during my marriage and after my divorce. I needed someone who was secure within himself and someone who wouldn't be intimidated by my intellect and success. Honestly, when Rashad came along, I didn't know what to expect because I wasn't really looking to get into a relationship with anyone during this time.

And, I also wasn't even really interested in the possibilities of getting to know him at first. My last break up was still fresh and the last thing I needed was another failed relationship.

I didn't want another binding soul tie on my hands after God delivered me while on my spiritual sabbatical. He washed my sin-sick soul from all the other soul ties I created and the heartache I suffered from over the years. God taught me about self-worth and what it means to love myself first before anyone else could love me. I learned who I was in God and that I was fearfully and wonderfully made!

> *Psalms 139:14 I will praise thee; for I am fearfully and wonderfully made: marvelous are thy works; and that my soul knoweth right well.*

God took away my desire and appetite for wanting to sexually please my flesh. I was finally content and happy in who I was in the natural and in the godly woman I'd become. This experience reminded me of my first experience with God, when I received the gift the Holy Ghost! I remember the feeling I felt on the inside was like no other feeling I'd ever felt before. I knew a change had taken place in my mind, body, and soul! I felt like a new person and I was free from the chains of my past! And Rashad, couldn't have met me at a better time! God's timing is always perfect and right on time!

Throughout our courtship, we got to know one another very well. We spent a lot of time together. Despite my busy life, I made sure that I set aside time to talk to Rashad or see him daily. The one thing that we had in common that drew us closer was the fact that we both lost one of our siblings. He lost his older sister and I lost my little brother within a year of one another. Just from the conversations alone regarding our losses, we were able to form an unbreakable bond. And it was during this time that Rashad told me he loved me for the first time. We fell in love at the same time I believe, but I would not utter those words before him! My former Bishop once told me that if a man tells you he loves you first then you got him!

Early on into the relationship Rashad started coming to church with me on a regular basis. This also, was important to me because being the woman of God that I was, I wanted my Pastor's discerning eye to discern his spirit. Except for the Birdman, I usually would never bring guys I was dating to church, but it was something different about Rashad. He loved God and because of this, he would have to go through God to get to my heart. I remember about five to six months after we started dating, my Pastor told me about this vision God showed her. In the vision, she saw Rashad and me walking down the isle of our church in our wedding. Of course, I was super excited and in being excited I still had to be cautious not to allow myself to get lost in him. What I mean by this is, I had to remain true to myself and the things that God imparted into during my spiritual sabbatical. I'd made far too many mistakes by diving headfirst into the wrong relationships and giving my all to men that had no good intentions with my heart and to men who didn't deserve me.

I experienced feelings of effervescence throughout the courtship. Rashad lavished me with nice gifts and trips from time to time. He used his charm to tell me how beautiful I was every day. He really knew how to make a bad day turn into a good day. Love was in the air! I started imagining what it would be like to spend the rest of my life with him. The big "M" word started surfacing in our conversations leading up to our first-year dating anniversary. He shared with me how he'd been praying for a wife and that he was pretty sure God sent me into his life for that reason. But I knew God also sent me into his life to introduce him to another side of God he hadn't experienced before, and that was God's presence living on the inside of him. He needed to be baptized in the Holy Ghost. God wanted to complete what he started in him. Rashad was so open to the things of God. He was willing to do whatever it took to soar to new heights in God. His love for God and his hunger and thirst for righteousness is what made me fall in love with him.

I didn't have to question his love for me because he showed me every day. Since we decided to talk about marriage, we went window shopping for engagement rings. We went to many different stores and I tried on a bunch of rings. Rashad asked me to narrow my choice down to five rings and then choose the one I wanted the most. The one I wanted the most was the most expensive, but it gorgeous and I loved this ring! I wasn't for sure if Rashad would even get the ring. Either way, he had five choices to choose from. I trusted his judgement and his ability to know what I liked and didn't like. And plus, God told me in His word in:

> *Psalms 84:11: For the Lord God is a sun and shield: the Lord will give grace and glory: no good thing will he withhold from them that walk uprightly.*

I didn't always dot every "I" and cross every "T" but the one thing I did know is, God knew my heart and He knew I wanted the expensive ring! LOL!

Ring shopping meant a proposal of some sort was coming. There was no way for me to prepare for this because I didn't know when he would pop the question. We'd only been together for about a year and a half. I always wondered if Rashad was thinking the same thing as me when it came to how long we'd been together. Six whole months passed since we'd gone ring scouting. I wasn't sure if he'd changed his mind about marriage or not because it hadn't come back up in any of our latest conversations. I began to get nervous. And then one night, Rashad called me and told me to get dressed and to wear something nice because he wanted to take me somewhere special for dinner. Now we'd been on a bunch of dinner dates with Rashad, but those dates were never set up the way he set this one up. I would normally arrange all our dates and he would just agree to go. He was not a hard man to please at all. This was another reason I loved him so much!

On the day of the special dinner date, I found something nice to wear. I got dressed and waited for Rashad to come get me. It seemed like it took forever but he finally arrived around 8pm and we headed out for our date night. He took me to Pappadeaux's Seafood Restaurant. I absolutely loved seafood! This restaurant was the place of our first official date. I had no clue of what was in store for me. We pulled up to the restaurant, Rashad let me out in front, and told me to go and add our name to the waiting list while he parked. I found us an outdoor table to sit at while we waited for our name to be called. We made small talk while waiting 45 minutes to be seated. You could tell it was summertime because there were so many people out that evening enjoying the nice cool night breeze.

I noticed Rashad fidgeting around a lot, like he was nervous about something. He excused himself from the table to go to rest room. He came back after about 10 minutes. As I was getting up to move out of the way so that he could sit down, Rashad pulled a little black box out of his pocket. I asked him what it was. He turned towards me and popped the box open and asked me to marry him! I was flabbergasted by his gesture! He was so smooth with it too! He didn't have time to get down on one knee because I jumped up and said YES! He got up out the chair and placed the engagement ring on my finger. It was the exact ring I wanted! I knew God was going to give me the ring I wanted! Come on here, God! He did that! I hugged Rashad's neck so tight. I could not believe he'd just proposed to me!

Our table buzzer went off and we were escorted to our table. On our way to our table we were telling the other restaurant employees and patrons, we'd just got engaged. Everyone was cheering and congratulating us! I felt as if I was sitting on top of the world and I could not stop smiling. My baby, my man, my best friend, and my lover decided he wanted to spend the rest of his life with me. I knew then at that moment that this was the reason why god wanted me to sacrifice my way of doing things to get a man. I now understood why god asked me to give him that year. He was preparing me to become a wife, and not just any wife, but a godly wife who was going to marry Rashad. Also, a wife that would know how to pray for her husband when things weren't so pleasant and when things got rough.

I remember this one conversation I had with an old friend about the "right one." I asked this friend how I will know when the right one comes along that's tailor-made for me. And the old friend told me I would just know. I knew when Rashad and I started dating that he was the one, but I didn't want to rush things. My confirmation was the dream my pastor had and that was all I needed. We had a few drinks with our food to celebrate this happy occasion. The sacrifice and one-on-one time with god were well worth it for this moment in time.

New Beginnings

I always knew there was a pot of gold at the end of my rainbow! I never lost hope in love or in waiting for that special someone. But this time around I knew it would be different because

Psalms 34:4 I sought the Lord and He heard me and delivered me from all my fears.

I knew God had someone else for me, but I had to give up my way of doing things. We sometimes hinder our own blessings by not totally surrendering to God and His will for our life. We won't allow ourselves to be made into vessels of honor because of the fear that lies within, that fear we feel when we are walking into the unknown. I'm glad I allowed God to work on me from the inside out. I felt like the caterpillar in the cocoon who had no choice but to go through the metamorphosis stage to become a beautiful butterfly. For me, I had to go through the fire to be transformed from a broken vessel of dishonor into a beautiful sculptured vessel of honor. You could no longer see the cracks and chips caused by the aches and pains of life. God now showcases me in the beauty and elegance that He molded me to be...

Here we were in the same month he proposed planning a wedding that would happen in August of the same year as our 2nd year dating anniversary. It all seemed surreal! Rashad and I had gone through a lot in the past year and a half to get to this point in our relationship. I was still in shock that he would be walking me down the aisle soon and I would become his better half. Being the hopeless romantic I am, I never counted out love's infinite possibilities. I always knew in my heart that I would give love a second chance. Rashad came into the picture and swept me off my feet. He wasn't the perfect guy, but I knew he loved me; so much, that he put a ring on it! LOL! We experienced a few hiccups during our time of dating. Hiccups I thought would tear us a part! What God put together, can't no man or thing come between. After eight years of being single, my Boaz was finally here. And I did not have to jump through hoops to get him. I simply decided to trust God with my whole heart. I was so tired of "spinning my wheels" and going nowhere with the men I dated before Rashad. I put my life in the best hands ever, and that was the hands of God!

We decided not to have a big wedding, but something small and intimate, with just family and close friends. There would be no wedding party, just us and our kids. Our pastors would officiate the wedding ceremony during Sunday morning service. The sermon topic was going to be about love. Excitement filled the air as I sat and had my makeup done by a very good friend of mine. My wedding dress hung on the door under the plastic it was shipped in. Butterflies were circling in my stomach. I was so nervous I couldn't stop perspiring. We had to be at the church before 11am service began. I'd already packed my overnight bag, because after the reception ended, we were going to our honeymoon suite at the Marriot Hotel.

The kids loaded up the car and we rushed to the church. I started crying in the car because my dream had become a reality. We finally pulled up to the church. Service was just starting, and I had to hurry to get dressed. My future husband was already at the altar. The kids made a dash to the restroom to change into their wedding attire. Ten minutes later they were walking up the aisle. I had about two minutes to put on my headpiece and get to the doorway entrance. I was overtaken by emotion as I entered the doorway. Everyone stood up and the wedding music started playing. My soon-to-be husband was looking as handsome as ever and he started smiling when I entered the sanctuary. With my son standing by my side, we walked down the aisle. He handed me over to my soon-to-be husband and took his place behind him.

My magical moment had come, and I was ready to be joined to my king. We could not stop looking at one another. All the wrong choices in men, bad relationships, tears, heartaches, and pain were all worth this very second and moment. "You may now salute your bride!" He grabbed me so tight, pulled me close, and gave me the most meaningful kiss he'd ever given me. We could hear the cheers and claps in the background. The kiss finally ended, and our pastors announced us. "We present to you, Mr. and Mrs. Smith!" My husband and I grabbed hands and walked back down the aisle towards the door into the reception area. We were now one in the flesh and spirit.

I never thought anything good would come out of the relationship trauma I suffered over the years or my divorce. You know the saying pain is gain? Well I never understood what that meant until now. After my divorce I thought I lost my life. Not in the literal sense but in the sense of, my life as I once knew. Even though I never lost hope in finding love again, I never imagined it to come the way it did. The one thing I know to be true about God is that, He never gives us what we think we want. He always gives us what He knows we need. We must be willing to go through the process and have patience to endure the journey. Sometimes the journey is long and lonely. In my journey, I learned that even though I could not see God, He was always there leading me and directing my path. There were many obstacles to go around and many hurdles to clear. I stayed focused on the finish line and I was able to cross it. My former Bishop used to tell us for all the tears we cried, God had them stored in a bucket in heaven and we could cash in our receipts whenever we got ready. I cashed in all those teary receipts on this very special day! My bag was filled with love, happiness, and joy! My spirit was at peace because God blessed me with the person, He tailor made just for me. He put my heart in the hands of the king He chose for me. And we know when God chooses, it's forever!

Life Lesson

To all my single ladies and gents, this so-called single life is not all that it is cracked up to be. As you can see, in all my failed relationships, I never put God first. I was blinded by Satan's illusion of love. It wasn't until God removed the scales from my eyes that I was able to recognize true love through the eyes of God. Love is not an illusion, it is real. The journey God took me on may not be the same journey He takes you on. But in your journey, seek the heart of God to see what He is saying regarding you and your love life. Let go of your past relationship baggage and allow yourself to be healed and made whole before you get into your next relationship. For you to be someone else's happiness, you must find happiness in God first and then within yourself. God must become your first love. If you don't take the time to get with God without all the distractions in your life, you will find yourself in a repeated cycle of failed relationships like me. I wrote about my experience to offer you hope, and to let you know that there is a silver lining in every cloud. Now go get with God because your true love awaits!!!!!

> *Rev12:11 And they overcame him by the blood of the lamb, and by the word of their testimony; and they loved not their lives unto the death.*

About the Author

My name is Sharee, I am in my mid-forties, currently residing in Atlanta, Georgia. Born in St. Louis, MO, I gained a love for writing through the many different books I read from my adolescent days to my teen years. I started out with poetry. As time continued and as I began to experience life, the thoughts of writing a book became more and more real to me.

I sat down and began writing, not a poem this time, but something much deeper and personal. I didn't stop writing until I birthed my first book, "This So-Called Single Life". This book journey's through my life after my divorce, detailing real and true events. It deals with being single after a very grueling divorce, all while working, dating, and raising 3 children on my own. I share my dating pitfalls and life lessons that I learned along the way.

I am now remarried to a wonderful husband. We have a total of five grown children, in whom I love dearly, ranging in age from 17-23. In my spare time, I love to write, listen to music, and spend time with my family.

Thank you for allowing me to introduce myself to you. And I hope "This So-Called Single Life" touches and blesses your life in a fulfilling way.

Made in the USA
Columbia, SC
03 February 2020